WEBSITE PRODUCT MANAGEMENT

KEEPING FOCUSED DURING CHANGE

ISBN 978-0-9914320-3-5

Images by David Hobbs. Exceptions: museum image from Wikimedia Commons and the "define, implement, review cycle" image based on a Shutterstock image.

Thanks, and how this book came about

I'm not even sure the distinction was intentional, but I was brought into the World Bank as a *Product* Manager (and not *Project* Manager). I took the difference between product and project seriously and have been running with it ever since. Much of the core of my thinking is based on five years in the trenches getting a couple thousand sites (including both external web and intranet sites) into a single CMS at the World Bank. At least two internal rebellions over those five years not to mention planning a bunch of big rollouts with clients later, and my thinking has refined to what's in this book.

The term "product management" as it relates to the web is bubbling around out there, with much of it focused on web applications that customers pay a subscription to access (Freshbooks, Basecamp, Github, etc.) rather than an organization's web presence overall. Others who have used the term to look at a web presence as a product include Seth Gottlieb, Kristofer Layon, and Scott Sehlhorst. I hope this book accelerates the discussion.

After leaving the World Bank, I worked at WelchmanPierpoint, and working with Lisa Welchman and the team there informs this book. The first time I published anything more than a blog post on website product management was while at WelchmanPierpoint in a 2009 Scribd document. Similarly, Tony Byrne and the team at Real Story Group helped to formulate my thinking on the topic. Another way of stating this is that they tolerated my ranting about product management.

Thanks to Deane Barker, Janus Boye, Roger Cauvin, Carrie Dennison, Clinton Forry, Seth Gottlieb, Wiep Hamstra, Erik Hartman, Ilse Jonker, Kris Mausser, Matt Mullen, Alan Pelz-Sharpe, Heather Ratcliff, Michael Theodore, and Martin White for feedback on the book. Kathy Kehrli of The Flawless Word copy edited the manuscript. Thank you Lisa, Chloe, and Astrid.

A special thanks to Jeff MacIntyre, who provided lots of great insight from input on the subject matter to writing and book rollout advice.

About David Hobbs

David helps organizations focus their websites. Clients include the Centers for Disease Control, the Center for Global Development, Heritage Foundation, Jackson Lab, the Library of Congress, Marriott International, the MBC Group, Realtree Outdoors, Thomson Reuters, and the World Bank. David is also the author of *Website Migration Handbook v2.*

TABLE OF CONTENTS

INTRODUCTION
FOCUSING YOUR WEB PRESENCE OR INTRANET

You can do better. Yes, you personally. Wherever you are in the organization (or if you help build or run others' websites), you can strive to improve your web presence. And the way you can do this is by thinking of that presence as a product. Sometimes this eye toward improvement might mean simply pushing to better understand the business need of a potential new website feature. Other times you might attempt to roll out a change with a bit wider impact than the most obvious approach.

> Product Management … is not a job title or something that other people do. It's an element of the company's entire business model. — Steven Haines[1]

A web presence is not a typical product, since it is not usually something for sale itself. But product management is a discipline that clearly and holistically defines what is being offered (in this book, the product is the website or intranet) to potential and existing customers, and it is anchored in long-term business value. In the case of the web, your potential customers have a lot of other places they could go, so the competitive advantage is keenly important.

> Product management is the entrepreneurial management of a piece of business … with a goal of long-term customer satisfaction and competitive advantage. — Linda Gorchels[2]

1 *The Product Manager's Desk Reference*, Steven Haines, 2009.
2 Transitioning from Engineering to Product Management, Linda Gorchels, Engineering Management Journal, December 2003

That said, most organizations' websites aren't focused on customer satisfaction and competitive advantage at all, frequently turning into bureaucratic dumping grounds. Consider two of the world's biggest companies, ExxonMobil and Apple, and the difference in their home pages.

Apple home page

Exxon Mobil home page

The Apple home page is clearly focused on the company's recently-released product, whereas ExxonMobil is more jumbled. As Scott Sehlhorst has noted, retailers understand "their website is the product that allows them to sell other products".[3] Apple as a company clearly has a singularly

3 http://tynerblain.com/blog/2009/08/24/product-manage-your-website/

strong product-driven organization, so it is not surprising that its website reflects a focused approach.

We tend to focus much more. — Steve Jobs

The screenshots above are the only ones you will see in this book. As we all know, home pages are becoming less important. Comparing them illustrates an example of focus but a key of product thinking of the web presence as a whole (even for an intranet, where the home page is perhaps more important). This texture of the website is nearly impossible to capture in a screenshot, and the opportunity for people entering your site from arbitrary pages is covered in "Rewarding the site visitor for being close" below.

The funny thing about a web presence is that it can quickly turn into a cabinet of curiosities[4], where we marvel at each separate site, section, or page for its novelty (or impressive newness), rather than looking at the focus of the entire web presence. This is understandable since the web is new and we want to show off our handiwork, like collectors showing off their specimens in the 16th century engraving below.

Is your site more of a curiosity museum?

But we as an industry need to advance to more focused sites, ones that are smaller and simpler.

---

4 http://en.wikipedia.org/wiki/Cabinet_of_curiosities

> ### Intranets and extranets too
>
> In general, the word "website" is used throughout this book, but that is primarily since there is no one good word to capture websites, intranets, and extranets. If you manage an intranet or extranet, you can almost always safely substitute "intranet" or "extranet" wherever "website" is used.

Small and simple

In many ways, product management is an attempt to keep your website as small and simple as possible. Of course, a massive organization will need to have a larger website than a sole proprietor will. But each organization should attempt to have its website as small and simple as possible. Note that here I am recommending both small *and* simple.

Small

This is how "physically" small your site is. The easiest metric to track is the number of pages. But this could also mean the number of topics in a topics list, integrations with other systems, sites, site sections, the number of PDFs, the number of languages, or even the size of each item (for example, the size of each page).

> A designer knows he has achieved perfection not when there is nothing left to add, but when there is nothing left to take away. — Antoine de Saint Exupery

For ideas on keeping your site small, see "Keeping your web presence small and simple" in Part 3.

Simple

A site could be simple yet huge. This gets to how the site and the backend is *organized*. If your entire site consists solely of press releases (even a million of them), then it is simple in one important way: its contents are all the same type.

Although of course we want variety and complexity on our site, there is a cost. Complexity comes in many shapes and sizes, including: content types, level of content structure, back-end functionality complexity, taxonomy complexity (depth, for example), and information architecture complexity.

The easiest way of reducing complexity is to not do something at all. For instance, you could decide to have your website in just one language rather than multiple languages.

Finding patterns and addressing the root issue rather than having a scattering of one-offs is a theme throughout this book, but in particular the whole section on streamlining explores how to treat common requests in a consistent manner. Also, it's easy to overcomplicate the implementation of your website in the first place, making it unnecessarily complex from the start. See Part 2:"Getting the bones right" for more.

Simplicity helps both in the cost of maintaining the site at high quality and also in helping the site visitor understand the site. This means that everyone can focus on the true needs of your site.

> "The busier life gets, the more value there is in simplicity as a point of competitive differentiation." — Arkadi Kulhmann, CEO of ING Direct USA[5]

Why focus?

Fundamentally, a focused web presence is easier for everyone. With a focused site, business objectives are easier to attain and the site is easier to manage. In addition, complexity only grows. Once the floodgate to low-quality changes is open, it's hard to close — furthermore, it is also difficult to undo low quality. For example, if you start launching one-off sites, it's hard to stop doing so — also, all those one-off sites are tough to rein into consistency later.

> As for simplicity, we think of it as the essence of the golden rule. Everyone wants to understand what is being offered or expected of them, and simplicity helps make that clear. It shortens the distance between people. — Simple: Conquering the Crisis of Complexity

---

5 http://www.siegelgale.com/blog/simplicity-war/

Focus for better business results

Focusing means that 1) you clarify what you are attempting to accomplish and 2) then reflect that focus on the website. The mere act of working to define exactly what the website is to accomplish is a significant step forward, so that you can align limited resources toward your goals. At a minimum, you can evaluate possible website changes against these goals.

Fundamentally, a more focused site means the site is focused on what the site visitor needs to accomplish. Anything else just confuses the path toward success for the visitor.

> Clutter is what happens when we fill a page with things the user doesn't care about. — Jared Spool[6]

A focused site is easier to manage

Even if a site didn't result in more success, a smaller and simpler website is easier to maintain. On the one hand this may seem counterintuitive since many think primarily of the raw storage cost. But, assuming we want to keep the website at high quality, more content, functionality, and complexity is just harder to maintain. In the case of content, much of what you create should be reviewed periodically, so that means that more content equals more effort to review. Every piece of functionality added to the system is one more thing that needs to be maintained (and potentially reviewed as the source of problems that inevitably arise).

There are several other reasons to focus a site. If you are creating less spurious content, then content contributors can concentrate on creating higher quality. Similarly, a more focused site, with clear locations for different types of content, probably means less probability that you create duplicate (or highly redundant) content. Finally, you are more likely to create backend tools that are easier to use (rather than tools to accommodate a variety of what-ifs and one-offs).

Complexity snowballs

Web presences often resemble Frankenstein's monster, with haphazard parts (sites, sections, topical pages, vanity sites, etc.) awkwardly sewn together. Once incoherent changes are made, it's difficult to stop. At least

---

6 http://www.uie.com/brainsparks/2011/11/04/clutter/

Frankenstein created something that had a clear number of parts (one head, two arms, etc.), whereas on a web presence, since it is so easy to add things, we usually just keep tacking more on. If you have allowed one group to create a one-off site, how can you say no to the next?

Aside from the incoherence that grows for the site visitor, another big problem occurs: it becomes harder and harder to make changes. This happens in two major ways: 1) resources are routinely used inefficiently so they cannot be deployed for new changes, and 2) when growth is made in an inconsistent way it is difficult to bring that growth back to consistency. On the first point, much of the "stuff" that's added to a website needs to be maintained if it's going to be high quality. This is especially true of functionality, which complicates the underlying technology and may make it harder to change. On the second point, it is always more difficult to move from less consistent to more consistent. That said, on the web matters are further complicated if different technologies are used since it just means that more systems have to be touched for changes.

Addressing blatant website focus problems

Many website problems for organizations are more in the backend than the front end. But some problems are laid bare for all to see on the public-facing website. Some of the most blatant website problems that we all see on websites include:

- Inconsistent branding, giving the visitor the "Am I still on the same site?" experience.
- Out of date information, leading the customer to question the overall accuracy of the site information.
- Inability for visitors to easily compare information across the site.
- Not being rewarded for being close (see below for more).

Of course there are plenty of narrow issues with specific pages as well, but, as we will discuss below (especially in "Long term and broad thinking"), product management is more concerned with site-wide quality. Sometimes this means defining and creating better templates or standards so that it's more difficult to create pages with these issues. But whatever the solution, product management attempts to rise above all the detailed issues to derive solutions that can be applied site-wide.

Reward your visitor for being close

As an industry we now accept that a large number of visitors first enter our sites directly at deep internal pages, rather than home pages or other top level pages. Although of course we hope that the visitor finds what they are looking for on this first page of their visit, this certainly isn't something we can rely on. That said, chances are that even if they aren't finding exactly what they are looking for on the first page, there is something about that content that is relevant on our site. And if we have that something special on our site, we'd like to provide them a quick path to that information. In other words, we need to reward our site visitors for being close.

For a simple example, consider the fact that I saw someone come to the Hobbs On Tech site by searching on "estimating website content migration" — the number one search result on Google was my post "Content Migration Burden: It's Not Just Automated or Manual." This is probably not the most relevant information on my site for what they were looking for. But this site visitor bounced from my site, probably never to return. Why would they know there is more relevant information on the site? I didn't reward them for being close.

Of course, big websites have even deeper difficulties in rewarding visitors for being close, both the root causes for the problems as well as how hard it is to address the problems. Here are some enemies of strong bottom-up browsing that I've seen in working with clients on the issue:

- **Duplication.** Duplication of content, extremely easy to occur in large organizations but also sometimes happens as workaround to technical issues, is detrimental all around, but in particular here since the site visitor may be confused by the duplication. If they aren't aware of the duplication, they may also inadvertently "lose" by starting their browse path in a context that is less useful.
- **Islands.** Ridiculously easy to occur when an organization itself is silo'd, islands of content are extremely disruptive to the site visitor who is starting their browsing from the silo that isn't relevant to them. Although sometimes duplication occurs across islands, even with unique content, islands of content can quickly result in visitors bouncing from your site.
- **Context resets.** I'm stunned by how often this occurs given how disruptive it is: the user comes to a page on a particular topic, and when they click for more information they have to start their search again. An example would be when you go to a product page for an item you just

purchased, and then when you click for the manual you have to start the search again on the support site.

- **Context leaps.** A bit more subtle (and probably only relevant for extremely large sites) than just plain resetting the context entirely, context leaps occur when the user is forced to select a next page that is either much more specific or much more general. An example would be if I searched for birds, came to a photo of a bird in Alaska, and could only browse from there to photos or Alaskan wildlife (but not just more birds).

- **Dead ends.** Nothing quite says "go away" to your site visitor than a dead end page: one that either has no useful links at all or that pushes you into an infinite loop of clicks.

- **Old relationships.** A piece of content is created in a moment of time, probably with links that are useful at their creation, but after publishing those links may no longer be the most relevant. Ideally these relationships are updated as new content is added.

- **Not having the information the user wants.** Years ago a client of mine called me in since they were really upset that their content wasn't appearing at the top of the Google search results, yet those that were at the top were referencing my client as the definitive source. The problem: the source organization didn't have a page specifically and only on the information that people frequently asked for. So you need to make sure you have content properly focused as well.

- **Low-quality information.** Low-quality information means that you have pages that are probably blocking the user from getting to the information they really want.

- **Unhelpful within-template context.** Pages for key content need to be carefully designed to ensure that the right contextual information is displayed right on the page. This can even include links to background or other key documents on particular topics.

Having a focused site helps to ensure that these issues are limited. For example, having a more focused site means that it is easier to put content in the right place so that duplication is less likely to occur and is more obvious if it does. Similarly, islands are less likely to occur if the process of creating new sites or site sections is streamlined appropriately (in other words, easy to create a site in a consistent way, but only if it meets minimum standards).

Another way of looking at this is that we want to control where problems are inserted into the website in the first place. This is a key theme throughout the book.

> **Reality check: how focused is your web presence?**
>
> - Is your website an appropriate size?
> - Is your site overly complex?
> - Does your website reward visitors who arrive at your site "close" to the information they really need?
> - When comparing areas of your website, is your brand portrayed consistently?

Hidden problems

Since we are tempted to think of websites as shiny objects mostly worthy of admiration, we may also be tempted to think that we can quickly understand a website's problems just by informally inspecting it. This is rarely the case. For example, I have had the following occur a few times recently on an initial call with an organization: Me: "Your site looks quite focused". Client: "Thanks, but you actually weren't looking at the most important section of our site" (referring to a section that I didn't even find in my initial tour). In other words, although in "What is website product management?" we looked at examples of where the site visitor can blatantly and quickly see problems, there are many more obscure problems that are not in the least bit obvious to visitors:

- Insufficient calls to action for desired actions
- Completely hidden sections of the site
- Related to the above section, insufficient cross-selling (which may be of benefit to the site visitor as well when they are close to the information they really would like to see but do not know is there)
- The inability internally to execute on immediate tactics that would improve the site (a clear example would be a cumbersome publishing process — see "Content publishing" in the section on streamlining common activities in Part 3)

Fundamentally, to evaluate the effectiveness of a website, especially as a whole, we have to evaluate against the business needs. More specifically, we have to evaluate against the strategy that the organization has committed to executing. Also, to truly evaluate the effectiveness of a site, we have to look across the entire site.

Product manage for better focus during change

Website product management is **management of change to keep the entire web presence focused over the long term**. This is accomplished by:

- Thinking about the website as a product, in particular starting with the business needs and always thinking long term and broadly about potential changes. See Part 1: "Product thinking".
- Getting the bones right, making sure you are maximizing impact in your implementation and effectively engaging stakeholders to define (and not "gather"!) requirements. See Part 2: "Getting the bones right".
- Committing to a process of ongoing change, both streamlining those activities that are common (like publishing content) and having a recurring process to make deeper changes. See Part 3: "Ongoing change".

The rest of this book gets into more detail about exactly what product management is and how to do it, but first let's compare other PMs that you may be tempted to conflate with product management.

Comparing the PMs

The purpose here isn't to form a rallying cry for people to start calling themselves "product managers," rather it is to make sure that website product management is *covered* by your organization. Let's start by looking at the driving questions of each of the main three PMs:

- Product Management: How do I maintain focus and high quality across the entire web presence over time?
- Project Management: How do I keep my project(s) on time, within budget, and in scope?
- Program Management: How do I maintain a portfolio of projects running effectively?

Product management is looking long term over the entire web presence, with a primary focus on features. The whole reason to take that approach is to maintain high quality and focus across the web presence over time. See "Maximize impact" in Part 2 for more on why the focus is on features.

Project management is concerned with making projects happen on time, under budget, and within scope, necessarily with a concentration on tasks. The time horizon is the duration of current projects (with a drive to *complete* them), and similarly only a part of the web presence is considered (the site sections affected by the projects currently being managed).

Program management is looking at a portfolio of projects. The time horizon is fiscal years or other budget planning cycles, and program management is probably concerned with systems beyond the web presence.

Types of PMs			
Type of PM	**Time horizon**	**Extent**	**Primary focus:**
Product	Long term	Entire web presence	Features
Project	Current project(s)	Part of web presence	Tasks
Program	Fiscal years	Beyond web presence	Projects
Each PM is important, but product management is critical and often missing.			

There are other PMs as well, such as Portfolio Management (for example, managing a portfolio of products), but the primary roles for web teams that I see at organizations are project and program management. An entire section of this handbook covers the need for product management to think long term and broadly, since this is so important to product management (and also unique compared to the other PMs).

The title "product manager" isn't enough

Sometimes organizations have product managers to manage various separate digital products (for example, different magazine titles). Just because you have product managers does not mean that you are doing overall website management as this handbook is promoting. In fact, individual product managers without overarching product management can lead to more fragmentation.

Other product management

Your organization of course may already do product management for your core products. The *Product Manager's Desk Reference* by Steven Haines says, "Like the physician, the primary function of the product manager is to choose the correct response to rapidly changing, complicated conditions, or in the best circumstances, to be able to anticipate and lead change." So at its core, managing a website as a product is similar to managing a more traditional product. There are some things that make website product management unique as compared to more generic product management (although of course there are other types of product management that share many of the characteristics below):

- Websites aren't a single thing (or even service) that is sold.
- Other products have a more direct lifecycle with respect to the buyer.
- Backend users "have to" use the CMS. Don't think this makes your job easier. For one thing, different units within your organization may still try to get out of the system. Also, since people don't have a choice about which system they are using, they may have a bad attitude about the system in the first place.
- You know exactly who your stakeholders are for the backend users, so you should explicitly get their input.
- In many cases, using a CMS may still be a shift in understanding for people. The main problem this causes for the product manager is that people may not understand what they are getting into enough to even tell you what they want, until you give them something they know they don't want. One good way to deal with this tendency is to develop concrete use cases to review with users before choosing a CMS so they know more what's in store.
- Often people enjoy hands-on HTML or developing websites themselves. So you will have people upset with the tool for reasons that, by design, have been implemented with less control (for instance, no longer having control over the whole page).

Agile development isn't enough

Just because you do agile development doesn't mean that you are doing strong product management. That said, when I talk with organizations about website product management it is sometimes brushed aside since they already do agile. Here are some ways that agile isn't enough:

- Agile doesn't have much to do with judgement required to think broadly and long-term.
- Agile doesn't have anything to say about standardization levels of websites.
- Agile doesn't talk about streamlining day-to-day flows.

How to read this book

If you only read one part of this book, please read "Think broadly and long term" in Part 1 below. If you are like me and mostly skim books, then check out the call-out boxes, which often include checklists that you can use to quickly engage with the ideas. If you are about to undertake a big website change, then I recommend reading this book through Part 2: "Getting the bones right". If there isn't a large undertaking now, then I recommend checking out the section on ongoing change.

You just read the introduction.
Now take at least this one action:

Think about blatant problems of focus on your website, and how managing change better could help avoid these problems.

Summary of Introduction: Focusing Your Web Presence or Intranet

- Focus is important.
- You can help your organization better focus your web presence, intranet, or extranet (and throughout this book "website" is used but most applies to intranets or extranets).
- A key goal is that your website is as small and simple as possible.
- In addition to blatant focus problems (such as not rewarding site visitors for arriving at your site at the wrong page but "close" to where they need to be), you probably have lots of hidden focus problems as well.
- Website product management is **management of change to keep the entire web presence focused over the long term**.

Part 1
Product thinking

Product thinking allows you to better focus your site. Just like popular consumer electronics products have product managers to focus them, a website should be viewed as a product as well. To think of your website as a product, always start with business needs and look long term and broadly when considering changes to your web presence.

Your site isn't a model ship in a bottle

Perhaps the biggest reason that we don't think business first is that we are too focused on the idealized state of websites. In many ways, we think of our website as something like a model ship hermetically sealed in a bottle:

- We fixate on beautiful mockups that show exactly what we've always dreamed our site could be. But we don't think about how those pretty web pages could be maintained. For instance, when thinking a bit deeper about a mockup, we may realize we don't have enough resources to sustain them (for instance, with tons of topic pages).
- We focus on the launch of a website, looking at how clean and perfect the site is on launch day, rather than the long-term needs.
- We are much more likely to launch one-off sites (that can be pristine) rather than looking enterprise-wide at our needs.

Our website isn't hermetically sealed in a bottle at all. It needs to be seaworthy, ready to be steered into the exciting sea (our markets). Of course, it's not going anywhere without the crew or, if it's a sailboat, without the right winds.

But fundamentally we need to decide what kind of ship we need. A cruise ship? A racing catamaran? An aircraft carrier? A canoe? A tugboat? I find that even very large organizations sometimes compare themselves to very small sites, when the comparison does not make much sense except for general inspiration.

The metaphor of website-as-ship breaks down in one significant way: we are building the website as we are moving forward (not sailing the ship back to port first to make big changes). So it really isn't just about defining your website well at the outset (getting the "bones" right); it's also about making sure that it remains seaworthy as you continue working on it. But regardless of the type of site, it still needs to remain sleek enough to keep moving forward (even an aircraft carrier can move, even though it is huge).

Start with the business need

The only reason to have a website at all is to serve a business purpose. Of course, if you are not running a for-profit enterprise, then your organizational purpose may not be business per se, but for now let's consider "business first" to encompass the broader "organizational purpose first." The product manager must anchor all decisions on the business. Obviously here we are not talking about purely personal websites.

Say no to bingo

I'm sure you've played buzzword bingo before, throwing around the latest trends as things your website needs to address. Sometimes it's played to impress each other, and other times it's more of a crutch. Perhaps the biggest reason for jumping on the bingo bandwagon is that people are more likely to try to follow other organizations than they are to lead. As of the writing of this handbook, here are some example words to dig into (and not take at face value) when defining things in a business-first manner:

- Personalized
- Agile
- Big data
- "Like Amazon" (or some other organization with massively more re-

sources than your own)
- Responsive
- E-marketing
- Cloud-based
- API
- Multichannel
- Social
- Any platform-of-the-month

When I ask clients what their online strategy is, it often amounts to picking a random selection of these hot terms, winding up with things like "Responsive website enhancing our brand" or "Multichannel publishing to curate a personalized experience." But it's important to ground whatever you are doing on what your business needs. The list of above buzzwords are a means to a possible business end, but they are not the end in and of themselves (unless, for example, you are an API infrastructure company!). Identifying an audience, where they need to use your website, and what they need from the website may result in a mobile strategy. But even with the business need established, you still need to dive into exactly how you will address that business need with whatever general approach you will take. For instance, if you have a hospital system where people often get lost, then you have an entrance into a very concrete mobile solution. The product manager needs to define that business need and then see it through execution to deal with that issue.

Your website vision

By playing buzzword bingo, your organization is basically saying its website is like all others. But nothing could be further from the truth. Just like your organization is unique, your website has a unique role in enabling your organization's goals. Your site vision should be meaty and unique, more like one of the following:

- Build brand affinity via nesting and treating the customer as a partner.
- Better demonstrate the value of the organization to members through a consolidated web presence.
- Improve information production and management services to include versioning and rollback, auditing and reporting, and more structured content.

- Exert speed under pressure: fast publishing process for news across the region, including creating fast-breaking new sections, such that even under the highest loads site visitors get a fast browsing experience.
- Inform and educate the American public and its policymakers on the impact of policy decisions of the day.

Internal or External Focus?

Generally speaking the vision will be externally focused. Even in periods of transition, where the focus may be more internal, obviously the external site must continue to meet site visitor needs. That said, there are always tons of internal details that need to be worked out to implement even a straightforward external focus. It isn't enough to just declare where you want to go. Always consider what needs to happen internally when considering change.

Most of these would probably make no sense whatsoever at your organization, and that is the point: your vision needs to echo what your organization needs, and not what every other website (thinks it) needs. Look at the first vision, which was for an outdoor recreation company, even using the word "nesting" to indicate different types of animal nests. The third one is for a very large site, where the raw content management needs were paramount.

These visions are vastly different from each other, and your unique vision should anchor all the decisions you make on your website. The focus needs to be at the level of making these business goals happen and not solely at the tactical level of tools and bits to be flipped.

Some keys of a strong vision (pulled from the fuller list at *Website Migration Handbook v2*[7]) include:

- Most stakeholders say it's compelling, and widely communicated. If everyone says it's compelling, then perhaps it's too limp of a vision. That said, most stakeholders should agree that it's worthwhile, and it should be communicated broadly.
- Understandable by all. Stakeholders often don't understand what they are agreeing to, so the vision needs to be clearly communicated (including what the impact is to different stakeholder groups).

---

7 http://migrationhandbook.com

- Can help prioritize. Especially for product management, one of the keys of a vision is that it is precise enough, and takes enough of a stand, to help prioritize the various day-to-day decisions.
- Achievable. One of the things that can kill confidence is overselling, so the vision must be achievable.

Vision depth

Since we need to look broadly (we'll get more into that later), we need to get a lot of people to understand our vision. This means that we have to go beyond the simple statement to actually make sure everyone understands what they are agreeing to.

In other words, we need to explore our vision and make sure everyone understands it. One tool to use in order to help communicate this vision is sliders to indicate how deeply you will support different aspects of your vision and also ensure that you maximize the value you are bringing.

Consider the vision for an organization that needs to emphasize its national ranking (for example in a customer satisfaction survey), be user-focused, and evolve over time (bootstrapping from where it is now). In order to explore the vision, a first step can be to define different levels for each of these aspects of the vision. For example, nationally ranked could be broken down into levels of support, starting with those that are easier in the short term to those that are higher quality yet more effort:

Example: depth of vision		
Depth of support	Ease of implementation	Resulting quality
Emphasize ranking on a limited and ad-hoc basis	Easy	Low
Emphasize rankings on every page (through global templates)	Medium	Medium

Comprehensive (every page individually targeted with a reason why the information on that page is reflective of a nationally-ranked organization)	Hard	High
Example depth of support for an organization that wants to emphasize that it is nationally ranked		

Emphasizing the fact that you have a choice, and can modify what you are attempting over time, a visually effective way to illustrate the depth that you are attempting can be shown like this:

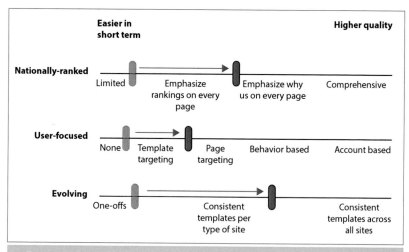

Example method of showing the scale of vision depth

In this case, the chart is representing how far to take each of the three pillars of their transformation (light brown being where they are now, and darker brown where they are attempting to be in the near term), and this quickly captures the fact that, for example, the need to evolve over time will be more of a priority than being user-focused in the near term.

> **Reality check: Do you have a business-driven vision?**
>
> - Have you defined the vision?
> - Is your vision based on business needs or more based on personal desires or chasing trends?
> - Is everyone inside your organization clear about the business goals of your web presence?

Hierarchy of stakeholders

When maintaining, improving, or radically changing your website (or the underlying platform), there are lots of stakeholders involved. Also, the stakes are high since it's really easy to implement things in a way that is not flexible or otherwise doesn't really serve the organization well. One problem is the temptation to oil the squeaky wheel, giving undue attention to power users when basic CMS users and external site visitors are more important.

But the only reason to have a website is to serve business goals (or, if you aren't running a business per se, your organizational goals). Obviously here I am not talking about personal websites that do not have business goals.

Any organization's website should be viewed (and managed!) as a product. This means that everything on the site should be geared towards your organization's (non-web) goals. So when deciding on what to do next on your website, it should always be viewed through the lens of your business goals.

External visitor needs should be prioritized over any CMS (backend) users, and basic CMS user needs should be prioritized over power user needs. But they all need to be anchored by the business goals. So the starting point should be the business goals. Instead of just listening to the clamor of requests coming in and prioritizing by stakeholder group, ideally you define goals and then prioritize your work program to move toward those goals.

Hierarchy of stakeholders

Better engagement is discussed in Part 2. See "Who are the relevant stake-holders?" in particular.

If you take only one action to
START WITH THE BUSINESS NEED....

Refine your vision if you have one clearly defined. If not, then make a stab at one. Then make sure to touch upon that for any change you are considering making to your web presence.

Think broadly and long term

Thinking long term and broadly is perhaps the most important aspect of product management, so pay special attention here. Fundamentally, any change has the possibility of eroding the website, either over the long term (for instance, something that is difficult to maintain) or in creating lower quality (for instance, implementing something that erodes brand consistency). Of course, change is also a must, so later on we look specifically at always phasing improvements and also streamlining things for common and important tasks (like routine content publishing). That said, a backdrop for all of this is the need to think both long term and broadly.

Groups willing to pay for their features

Since looking broadly and long term is so important when managing your website as a product, let's start with one type of situation that can easily devolve into thinking narrowly (for a particular group requesting a feature) and short term (looking simply at the short-term costs).

> I wish developing great products was as easy as writing a check. — Steve Jobs

Following are some reasons to not prioritize changes that groups are willing to pay for:

1. They aren't really paying the full cost. Sure, you might estimate the total development cost correctly, but are they even paying for simple maintenance of the feature? Upgrades? More subtly, are they paying for the extra regression testing now needed for features that aren't even directly related? Or the extra troubleshooting required for even what turns out to be unrelated issues?

2. Consistency of web experience for, you know, the site visitor. Not that this always seems to matter much in internal discussions, but is this better for the site visitor? Sure, it might be a gee-whiz and exciting feature. But is it going to confuse the experience of the rest of the site? Even if you could conceptually make it consistent, will you have the time to implement it in a way that's consistent?

3. Not implemented in an extensible way. If a particular group is commissioning a new feature, chances are they are thinking about how it needs to work for their site. The cost they are willing to pay will reflect that. So then you implement something (perhaps partially under the guise that this could be a "pilot" of a new feature), and other teams want it. Well, now the cost has actually gone up since not only does the feature need to be implemented anew for the rest of the site, but the feature needs to be retrofitted into the site that initially got that feature.

4. Not implemented in a technically consistent way. If only a particular group is getting a new feature, then even the technical team will be tempted to take shortcuts to get it in as directly as possible. This may seem innocent since, hey, only this group cares about it. But actually adding any complexity to your system just adds to the Frankenstein nature of your implementation. This means that as you are adding features you are just adding heft that may eventually grind your ability to implement new features to a halt.

5. Limited resources anyway. Alas, you are only dealing with limited resources anyway. Maybe you can throw an external development team at the problem. But even if you are able to do that, what about the core team's coordination cost? This just means they won't be able to spend time on items that *all* groups want.

Obviously, sometimes special functionality needs to legitimately be developed. But consider the factors above before providing a new feature, and never just because a group is willing to "pay for it".

Broad thinking

Broad thinking is considering all the factors needed to successfully deliver and maintain site capabilities or characteristics (and how to deliver the strong functionality across all stakeholder touch points).

There are certainly some overlaps with long-term thinking here, so let's concentrate on these aspects of breadth:

1. Breadth of **stakeholders** required to implement the functionality
2. Breadth of **teams** that need to coordinate to deliver the capability
3. Breadth of stakeholder **touch points** when stakeholders interact with the capability or characteristic

We will look at each in turn.

Breadth of disciplines

Pretty much any team has its biases, and chances are there is a strong reason for that bias (a company selling lots of products may need very strong taxonomists for example). But whenever approaching any particular problem, you need to consider: which disciplines are required for the current problem I am trying to solve? Here are some of the types of disciplines /

stakeholders you need to consider:

- Taxonomy
- User-centered design
- Content strategy
- SEO
- Site search
- Project management
- Systems administration
- Front-end development
- Back-end development and database administration
- Various disciplines required for your specific subjects (for example, financial analysis for a brokerage)
- Writing for the web

The point here isn't that you need to hire a team packed with all these stakeholders, but that you need to always think, "If I am trying to get to point A, what disciplines do I need in place to accomplish (and sustain) that?"

Breadth of teams

This one is very important yet won't take much space in this handbook: all the *teams* needed should be involved as well. Every organizational structure is different, but even if we consider the various teams directly responsible for different websites, when looking at a particular capability all the teams should be considered. So if there are two major product lines, and each product line is managed by a different team, then if a capability that both teams may use is being considered, both teams should be involved in the discussion (see "Engage for better requirements" in Part 2 for more).

Breadth of digital customer touch points

When designing very locally, it is easy to overlook the fact that this is not at all the way that stakeholders interact with your site (unless it is very small). For example, consider the simple case of someone purchasing a product:

1. Via mobile phone, do a Google search on a term that the customer is interested in buying.
2. Wind up on some page on your site.
3. Get to the page they are really interested in (refer back to "Reward

your visitor for being close" in the introduction) — note that this may mean the site visitor conducts a search rather than browse.

4. Go through the sales funnel.
5. Receive the product.
6. Have a problem with the product, and contact you.
7. Happy (hopefully!) customer rates your product.

Looking very narrowly we might skip right to the page in step 3 above, focusing on clearly describing why someone should buy the product. Obviously this is crucial, but it isn't relevant if no one can find it (or if everyone complains later that they can't find the support materials they need on your website).

When looking at making any change, consider your various possible digital touch points, which may include:

- The main corporate site
- Other sites: country sites, product sites, microsites
- RSS and other APIs
- Emails
- Different language versions
- Different devices
- Social media
- Site search
- External distribution

It's not just the website

For convenience, the word "website" is used throughout this document, but as mentioned earlier this book applies to intranets and extranets as well. In addition, other web-related touchpoints (such as those listed above) should always be considered when looking broadly at your site. For an obvious example, consider how the content will flow outside your main site and be distributed. Although this is becoming more important, the problem is not new. Take, for example, RSS feeds, which need to be carefully product managed as well (see "Designing RSS Feeds for Information-Heavy Organizations: Non-Web Distribution of Your Content" on the WelchmanPierpoint blog).

Reality check: How much of the website are you talking about?

I frequently talk with people who are concerned with improving their website, only to discover that they are only discussing (or undertaking to change) a tiny portion of the overall website from the site visitor's perspective. As just discussed, part of product thinking is to look at all the parts of the website that the customer will be interacting with. So a key question is: are you looking broadly enough at your web presence? To answer this question, consider the following:

- What are the total number of pages of the web presence as a site visitor could view it (across all sites, micro sites, and sections)? So count up the pages in the online help, document repositories, and other parts of the site.
- Of the total number of pages exposed to the site visitor, how many are you attempting to manage as a product? What is the percentage of the total?
- Does this division overlook key opportunities for your business?

Sometimes managing parts of the web presence completely differently makes sense, but this should only be done when you are sure that you will have the resources to maintain them over the long haul (or have a plan for deleting them fairly quickly). That isn't reason enough to product manage them differently. Two reasonable reasons include:

- The site sections have completely different audiences, with limited or no cross-selling and content overlap. For example, I worked with a very large company that basically acted as a hedge fund of other companies, and major divisions (brands) dealt with completely different audiences with very limited cross-selling across them.
- The separating site requires a reasonable feature set that is complex, required, and only needed by one group. For example, at the World Bank the HR group requested some security-related functionality for the intranet that only they cared about. In hindsight, their portion of the intranet should have been implemented separately with another tool. The reason? Every time problems arose in the system, we had to separately test their security functionality. So the additional complexity raised the maintenance cost but the World Bank did not significantly gain by having that functionality on the common platform.

When looking at the scope of product management (and specifically whether to treat some sections of your organization's web presence separately), consider the advantages of product managing as a whole vs. separately:

Product managing sites / site sections together or separately	
Together	**Separate**
<ul><li>Ability to cross-sell and reward the visitor for being close</li><li>Easier to be cost-effective</li><li>Strong brand re-enforcement</li></ul>	<ul><li>Separate brand can have a unique look (but it has to truly be a unique brand for this to make sense)</li><li>Separate portion of the site can implement unique functionality</li><li>Easier to culturally implement (this is NOT reason enough!)</li></ul>
In general, the advantages of product managing a wider scope outweigh managing in a more piecemeal fashion.	

Long-term thinking

Long-term thinking is creatively thinking how capabilities or site characteristics will be maintained over time (as well as new instances and decommissioning over time).

Let's break this down into its components:

- **Creatively thinking.** Product management isn't just taking orders from stakeholders. Product management frames problems and opportunities, perhaps completely shifting the conversation on an issue (see "Engage for better requirements" in Part 2 for more).
- **Capability or site characteristics.** Product management is shepherding in two aspects of a site: capabilities (whatever a particular organization is considering for its site, from mapping, APIs, social sharing, within-organization content sharing, etc.) and site characteristics (for instance, consistency across the entire web presence).
- **Maintained.** It's not much use to deploy something that immediately erodes. This can apply to content, a standard, or a new capability.
- **New instances and decommissioning.** If you are confronted with a

request to make a change to a particular piece of content, site section, template, or website, then how will the next request of the same type be addressed? If it will be considered as a completely new request, then you aren't thinking for the long term.

- **Over time.** The primary point of long-term thinking is that the impact of any change over the long term should always be considered.

As a flip side, if there is one thing that erodes website quality the fastest it is short term thinking. Unfortunately, given the immediacy and speed of implementing changes on the web (a good thing), this means that many organizations think they should be making whatever change crosses their path.

Example: short-term vs. long-term thinking

Joe makes your life difficult, because he is so consistently vocal and disapproving of the web program and pushes very hard for his unit's needs within your company. He is highly knowledgeable about the web, and is very technically capable. He just attended a conference on methods of exposing data, and was particularly interested in a technique to display data in a table. All he needs is raw HTML access to one page.

Option 1: open up raw HTML editing (short-term thinking)

Joe is going to make your life a living nightmare if you don't provide this capability, and it is so easy to provide (especially compared to the rest of his long list of requests). So you give him the raw HTML access. These are the advantages of this approach:

- Joe is somewhat happy for now.
- You've been wanting to try new ways of visualizing data, and someone is willing to try it out on their dime.
- It really didn't take much effort on your part to deliver this request for Joe.

Assuming you simply gave this functionality to Joe, there are a lot of long-term issues:

- There is a very high probability that Joe will ask for this capability again for other pages (magnifying all the problems below).

31

- Other stakeholders, without the same technical skills, will ask for the same possibility. Since Joe is just responsible for his unit's site (and he is probably already overextended), this will just mean more effort on your part since you will either have to fend off further requests or give in and then have to provide training and support.
- Although it is nice to test new features, without doing it in a methodical way there is a reasonable probability that the way that the feature is developed for this single site would not apply enterprise-wide.
- It is more difficult to transform the entire site later, with this forever being a one-off to deal with (for instance, if you later wanted to be able to serve all pages at a very narrow width then this page may have to be dealt with separately).
- If you specifically wanted to provide a data table capability, then there is one more exception that has to be dealt with.
- There is no easy way of consistently checking / monitoring for quality.

Option 2: long-term thinking

Given the importance of creativity in responding to requests, there could be a lot of ways of thinking about this long term. But to flesh out this example, let's consider that we do the following:

- Ask Joe to raise this issue as part of your ongoing improvements program (see "Always phase changes" in Part 3).
- Instead of responding to the specific request (raw HTML access), address the deeper problem (rendering data tables).
- Involve other stakeholders in the discussion.
- Discuss more broadly what it means to have strong data.
- Provide a mechanism that allows stakeholders to add data tables (without opening up the HTML).

There is a significant downside to this approach: Joe is probably upset with you right now. Also, in the short term you don't have a new data table display method. But you would have several long-term benefits, including:

- All stakeholders have a means of adding data tables.
- You have had the chance to discuss what data means to your company, and hence perhaps you have charted out more of a trajectory for continuing improvements.

Here we looked at one possible response. But there really is a scale of possible responses (from the one that is easy now but worst in the long term to the one that is the most difficult to install now but best over the long term):

1. Open up the HTML for a page.
2. Provide a tool for more flexible tables.
3. Provide data tables.
4. Provide data infrastructure that includes data tables.

In general, the product manager is always balancing the long-term benefits, creatively finding the right level of response to any specific request (more in "Always phase improvements").

Other types of short-term thinking

Short-term thinking isn't just about creating one-offs, although it is the most obvious and most important issue to be alert to (and is covered more in the standards section of this handbook). Here are some examples of short-term thinking that aren't about creating a one-off:

- Too much "what if" thinking. Over-engineered solutions are very common. In fact, one of the most frequent causes of an ossified system is considering too many cases early on. Since you can never truly future-proof (although all of the suggestions here for product managing your implementation reduce the problems), there is little reason to implement structures that you *might* use sometime in the future. Furthermore, too much "what if" thinking can mean that you overbuy your technology in the first place. Another common example of an over-engineered solution is a complicated taxonomy, which can result in low-quality tagging (see the blog post "The metadata sweet spot"[8]).
- Implementing something at all. Sometimes, the best response to a request is "no" or at least "not now". The suggestions in "Always phase improvements" help to ensure that you only implement the highest-impact changes, but fundamentally it's important to remember that you don't need to implement some requests at all.
- Assuming things will always be the same. Content in particular is often created as if it will be useful forever. Of course, there is evergreen con-

---

8 http://hobbsontech.com/content/metadata-sweet-spot

tent, although that should be reviewed over time (unless it is archival or historical in nature).

- Considering anything "done". Recently when working with a client on sequencing functionality into a website, they wanted to know when each package of functionality should be complete. I pointed out that a better approach was that these packages would continue to improve over time, and to start inching forward on those changes. By considering things done you don't consider the possibility that they were not implemented in a way that satisfied the stakeholders.

Cost over time

One way to think long term is to think about long-term cost. This approach is more descriptive than a detailed estimate. We'll look at two components of long-term cost:

- The cost of future instances
- The cost of making a site-wide change

The cost of future instances

Half of the product management battle is finding or creating patterns that emerge or are underlying individual requests. Diving right into an example, consider that you have created three one-off conference sites for your annual conference. Each one cost $50,000 to create, and then it took some time each year to get used to the nuances of the revised content entry approach. You now have this year's conference coming up. You have two options:

- Create another one-off conference site, and repeat that same pattern again next year, so $50,000 this year and then $50,000 next year.
- Create a standard site that can be replicated for future years. For the purposes of illustration, consider that it takes $60,000 to create the more extensible template this year, and then $10,000 next. This would mean that by next year you would have recovered your costs.

Here we are looking solely at cost, and in "The standards conundrum" we will look more at other advantages of standardization.

The cost of making a site-wide change

Sometimes you need to make site-wide changes — things like:

- Templating:
  - Changing your company logo
  - Changing a common term
  - Changing the color scheme.
- Navigation
  - Add a secondary navigation item to all pages across the site.
  - Change the navigation so it works better on some new device.
- Functionality
  - Improve content publishing preview across the entire web presence.
  - Add API access to all datasets exposed across the website.

How easy would it be to make a logo change across your entire site? If the answer now is "hard," then you may have created a bit of a fossilized site. Regardless of the answer, you need to ask that sort of question when deciding how to respond to any question. More specifically, the question is "Would responding to this request mean that it would make it harder to change the logo across the web presence later?"

Sometimes the changes are strictly across your entire web presence, but across all similar sites (in the case that your web presence has many separate sites — see "New site creation flow" in Part 3). This would include items like:

- Change the way all country sites aggregate the latest news
- Including a new left navigation item on every country site

As with all product management decisions, this is just an input into the decision of what to include on your site. Also as always, there will be conflicting inputs in making your decision (see "Factors in deciding the work program" in Part 3).

Long-term engagement funnels

As an example of thinking long term, consider long-term engagement funnels. Are you optimizing your web presence (not just your main website) for transactions or relationships? Given the immediacy of the web, especially in how easy it is to do stuff, it's easy to think short term. For instance, you may do something that increases the percentage of visits that people buy your main product (optimizing the single transaction checkout funnel). This clearly is important, but I would encourage you to think longer term, not just concentrating on the single transaction, but on what you are attempting to accomplish with site visitors over the long term.

If you consider a car rental company, they want people to rent cars with them. But it's clearly not enough to just make it easy to rent, since other factors (like price) may mean that people don't even consider their company for a particular transaction (when a competitor has a cheaper price). So rental car companies have loyalty programs that make it more likely to consider them and use them. The point is that this process isn't just about optimizing single transactions. Rather, it is about creating an affinity and predisposition to your offerings.

In addition to services companies (like the car rental company), this table gives a flavor of how other types of organizations, for example research and membership organizations[9], might think about their engagement funnel:

---

9 Also see *Maximum Engagement* by David Gammel, 2011.

Example engagement levels			
	Type of organization		
Engagement	*Research*	*Services*	*Membership*
Level 1 (shallow)	Aware	Aware	Aware
Level 2	Share	Purchase	Join
Level 3	Collaborate	Loyalty program	Participate
Level 4 (deep)	Effect change	Strong preference	Lead
Note that deeper engagement is long term and over time, not one visit.			

Each organization will have a different engagement funnel (for example research organizations have very different audiences and goals). The above table is an oversimplification, but hopefully it shows the type of variety between even types of sites.

Note that one of the main things you are looking for here is **amplification**. Let's take the example research institution funnel of aware > share > collaborate > effect change. Someone may first hear about your organization through a blog post that one of their colleagues mentions (they become aware). If they feel motivated, they will then share that post. If they collaborate with you, then they will be even more likely to spread your organization's message. Talk is cheap. What you really might want is to effect change, for instance perhaps changing people's day-to-day behaviors. At each stage, the impact of the engagement is stronger.

Really, you will almost certainly have multiple engagement funnels: **one per primary audience**. You may want different audiences to take different actions, all anchored by your overall website vision. A professional association may have separate interactions for students, professionals, and potential customers of these professionals. A product company may target consumers and businesses differently. Each particular organization is unique, and there is no plug and play audience list (and associated long-term engagement funnels per industry). For example, some think tanks target the general public and others do not, which means that the goals and engagement funnels are very different.

Drive website decisions using your long-term engagement funnel

As discussed above, business goals should drive all the decisions on your site. Looking at the engagement funnels is a concrete way of defining those goals. Decisions about your website should consider your engagement funnels:

- Are there some stages of your funnels (remember you will probably have one per audience) underrepresented on your web presence?
- Does every interaction either encourage 1) deeper engagement or 2) further engagement at the level the visitor is already at (and not bouncing out to some lower level of engagement)? Does every web page do this?
- Are there ways of measuring your engagement level?
- Are some levels overrepresented?

What engagement funnel would work for your type of organization?

Are you taking a product view?

To help clients navigate whether they are treating their website as a product, I have developed the following table — you can use the right side as a checklist to see if you are currently taking a product view.

Product thinking checklist	
NOT taking a product view	**Taking a product view**
Primary reason for undertaking a new feature, site, or content is whether there are staff (and budget) to undertake it.	Staff/budget only a part of the discussion, and long-term cost (and complexity for user) is always considered. Also, question whether this request is common enough that it should be streamlined (see "Streamline common activities" in Part 3).

Asking for clients (including internal clients) to give the requirements	▪ Shaping the requirements, based on current request and broader needs ▪ Working with clients to define requirements that can be delivered and tested in the near term ▪ Boldly surprising users with features they wouldn't know to ask for See "Engage for better requirements" in Part 2.
High frequency of one-off features, sites, or content	Steering requirements toward those that solve a wide range of stakeholder needs. See "Maximize impact" in Part 2.
Primary discussion around whether features delivered to requirements	Primary discussion around whether user (and organizational) needs are met. See "Start with the business need" above.
Narrow, silo, or discipline-specific perspective	Considering all stakeholders and all user touch points. See "Think broadly and long term" above.
Scheduling into the medium or long-term future for features that are known now	Setting up a process for ongoing improvements, including those that no one can currently foresee. See "Always phase changes" in Part 3.
Rewarding the squeaky wheels	Rewarding the truly important stakeholders. See Part 3: "Ongoing change."

Product thinking checklist: move to the right!

> **You just read THINK BROADLY AND LONG TERM.**
> **Now take at least this one action:**
>
> When considering any proposed change, at least note 1) the long-term issues you may be introducing and 2) any broader, higher-impact changes that are not being taken.

Summary of Part 1: Product Thinking

- Stop thinking of your site as a model ship in a bottle (focusing on static and idealized views of your site) and instead think of it as a seaworthy vessel (that has to always react to changes).
- Anchor every change on your business needs and vision.
- **Think broadly**, across all customer touch points, disciplines, and parts of your website, when considering changes.
- **Think long term**, considering how you can both maintain the site and also continue to make changes for the long haul.

PART 2
GETTING THE BONES RIGHT

I t's easy to make changes on the web. But we don't want a cancerous (out of control and malignant) growth. Instead, we want a web presence that makes some sense to our site visitors and is easy to maintain. We need to get the bones right.

Broken gets fixed. Shoddy lasts forever. — Jack Moffett

But we don't usually get the bones of our website right at all. We shun the mess website we have now only to create another mess on a new system (although it may take a year or two for the mess to appear). One of the most frequent problems when replatforming, for example, is attempting to do far too much with the website and underlying technology. This is a problem for two reasons. One, it is more difficult to implement more complexity in the first place. Two, you can wind up with an implementation so heavy that it crushes the breath out of your site. In other words, the implementation becomes so burdensome that all your effort goes to maintaining the original complexity rather than enabling continuing growth and improvement.

Instead of rushing to complexity in an attempt to keep up with the latest buzzwords or trying to finish a single grand launch, we should always be looking to isolate the real business need. In particular, we should focus on those aspects that are the most important to have as simple and small a site as possible.

The following table lists some problems people report with their web technology, and the real underlying problems.

Reported vs. real problems	
Reported problem	**Real problem**
Not flexible enough / can't keep up with trends	▪ Didn't define broad needs of the website enough in the first place. ▪ Too many one-offs from the start and over time. ▪ Overly-customized implementation.
Difficult to publish content	▪ Didn't prioritize publishing process from the start. ▪ Complicated the process to take into account infrequent special needs. ▪ Moved to a distributed publishing model without considering full impact.
Can't make routine site changes as quickly as needed	▪ Haven't properly streamlined or standardized common types of site changes. ▪ Didn't properly define a hierarchy of complexity for the site. ▪ Didn't identify and prioritize routine site changes in initial requirements.
Always attempt to tackle the root issues.	

When to get the bones right

There are several times when you need to try to structure things correctly:

▪ When changing the underlying technology
▪ When generally trying to make big changes, including trying to rein in previous changes that were not done in an ideal manner
▪ When confronted with what, on the face of it, appears to be a smatter-

ing of disjointed issues that represents a deeper pattern.

Let's consider the case of a CMS replatforming project. In that case, ideally we follow this process:

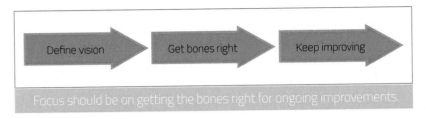

Focus should be on getting the bones right for ongoing improvements.

In this model, we first clearly define what business goals our website is serving. Next, we set up the "bones" of the overall system. Here, I don't just mean the right CMS, but things like: a) the right templating approach, b) the staffing commitment to maintain high quality, and the technology to match, and c) the resolve to keep improving, and to anchor our changes on the vision (and not the squeaky wheels). Only after the flexible structure of a growing skeleton do we move on to the improvement phase.

> You see, there's a murky space between the *idea* of content, and the hard *reality* of a content management system. — Deane Barker[10]

But that's not the way most organizations approach replatforming their site, which goes more like this:

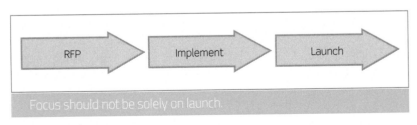

Focus should not be solely on launch.

In this model, we might not even really understand the problem before sending the RFP, in the hopes that the implementation vendors will also help in defining the needs (or worse, we may not have any desire to under-

---

10 http://gadgetopia.com/post/8821

stand the business needs). The implementation is focused on the launch, and we forget after launch. In addition, we might even focus on creating a new website entirely that looks slick but creates yet another silo. Perhaps the biggest problem: we thought more about what the site needs to look like upon launch and not how it needs to respond over time.

What are the bones?

One way to look at it is that the vision first needs to be set, then this ripples out to defining and implementing the bones of your web presence, and from there you can keep improving in phases (either as a part of a phased rollout on a new platform or on an ongoing basis). In the diagram below, each wedge represents an area that is needed for a website to function. The point here is less that this is exactly how you would break down the areas, but that at least these areas need to be covered. Each successive "wave" radiating out from the vision means more depth in both planning and implementing each of these areas. But organizations usually have pretty strong biases on what is important, and so planning and implementation often goes quite deep into one area at the expense of others. For example, since the technology is often the scapegoat, the entire focus of a replatforming may be on the technology. But without considering the people for example, you could implement technology that satisfies the technologists but not the individuals actually using the system (and so even with the shiny new CMS you wind up in the same mess again a few years later).

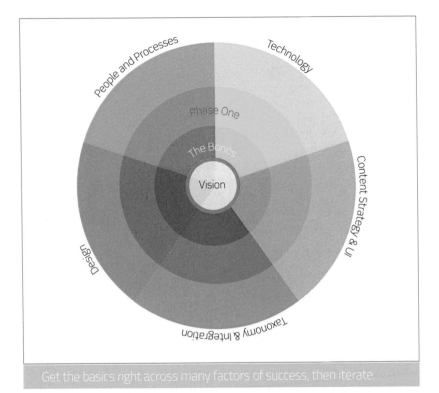

People and Processes

Technology

Phase One

The Bones

Vision

Content Strategy & UI

Design

Taxonomy & Integration

Get the basics right across many factors of success, then iterate.

A dramatic example of where the bones aren't right is when a company pushes toward distributed content publishing without getting the basics done first. What happens when the bones aren't right for distributed content publishing? Wide discontent and unmet business needs! This is serious yet happens often. Using the example of distributed content, consider some of the things that need to be in place:

- A very streamlined content publishing process
- Appropriate training and help desk support
- A clear understanding of content needs (who should be publishing, why, what they should publish, etc.) that is also widely communicated and understood
- Constrained design capabilities for each page
- A clear site and taxonomy structure to be publishing into
- Wide buy-in on the overall approach (for example, if part of the implementation involves "placeless" content that flows throughout the site,

then everyone needs to buy into that so they don't try to game the system to work otherwise)

This raises another important aspect of setting the vision: ensuring that the vision is implementable. There's no sense defining one that isn't implementable, so thinking through how you'll pull it off is important. For example, if the above isn't worth it to your company, then don't implement distributed publishing!

Of course, we have the technology to change "the bones" as we proceed, and so if you don't have the structures that you need you can certainly add them as you go along. This will be covered in Part 3:"Ongoing change" below.

Considering the different disciplines is important but not enough. We want to set things up to maximize impact.

Your CMS isn't the problem.

I'm frequently taken aback by blog posts that attack CMSes, or at least the CMS they are using. On the one hand, I understand it completely. For example, when working with a publisher recently, after just ten minutes of them walking through their system I declared, "I can see that this is unusable." On the other, the problem is rarely the CMS platform itself, and by attaching so much weight to the CMS, organizations may be led to believe that just swapping out the CMS will solve everything. Also, blog posts frequently state that a large organization has "adopted" some low-powered CMS, when really it is being used for an extremely small part of the organization's web presence — the skill comes in making things work enterprise-wide.

The problem boils down to the fact that most organizations don't figure out what they need their CMS to do. This extends to when some particular group gets a waiver to do a task fast and loose to implement something for their specific needs. Large web presences are complex (and usually have an entire ecosystem of systems, including multiple CMSes), so in no way am I attempting to oversimplify.

Let's look briefly at what makes up a CMS implementation:

- The underlying CMS itself
- The implementation of the CMS
- The content
- The surrounding ecosystem (like training)

All of these are much more intertwined than we usually want to let on, retreating back to our "camp" to criticize the groups we perceive to be problems. People with content hats criticize the tool (the CMS) while the technical people are pointing at the content owners saying they are like herding wild cats. Fundamentally, no one is taking into account that the living and breathing website is an ecosystem of many things, but fundamentally, people don't consider what their CMS needs to do. For example, the everyday publishing use case is critical but often overlooked (see "Content publishing"in the section on streamlining common activities in Part 3.).

The problem of not defining the CMS implementation clearly is that you wind up with Frankenstein's monster. Of course there are governance issues, but often the problem is that people don't even know what they are shooting for when selecting and then implementing the CMS. By bolting on extensions and customizations, we end up with something that can't be sustained. So the primary concern of website product management is features. The barrage of feature requests is constant, and so the person playing the product management role must be a confident decision maker. Also, this handbook lays out a structure to put in place to help in that decision-making process, so that it is clear to all stakeholders. The topic of requirements definition is covered in a future section.

Maximize impact

Product thinking means that we are anchoring on the business needs and looking broadly and long term at potential changes. To actually execute on that, we need to set up our web presence so that we can make high-impact changes.

Consider a new site request for a web presence (for an organization with a legitimate need for a suite of sites). There are two ways of setting things up: 1) each site being completely independent or 2) a site being based on a template (we'll get into more of the nuances in the coming chapter). Taking the RFP (or just requirements if internal) > Implement > Launch approach, we may be tempted to set up the site as a one-off. But this is far less powerful than identifying similar sites and implementing them in a templates manner. For example, if you have product micro sites, then it may make more sense to create them on a templated model. In that way, if you need to make broad changes (for example, a new menu item on every product page), then it is straightforward to do so.

Another example is making a one-off change to a particular piece of content where a change to the display template for a common content type would have far higher impact. For example, a change to a template to include a standard way of sharing the content on social networks is far more effective than offering such an option on a particular piece of content. An even higher-impact change would be a system-wide feature where sharing is implemented in a way such that it can be added to any page or content type. Of course, this approach also adds even more complexity / weight to the system, so it should be carefully considered before adding.

One of the reasons that product management is focused on features is that they have the possibility to have a high positive impact. However, they also have the possibility of significantly increasing the weight of the system. This table summarizes this thinking:

Probable impact and weight of additions		
Adding or enhancing _one_ of these	**Impact to the web presence at large**	**Additional weight to the system**
Feature	High	High
Standardized site type	High	Medium
Specific site	Medium	High
Standardized display template	High	Medium
Specific, single piece of content	Low	Low
Attempt to maximize impact when implementing.		

Other examples of functionality might be:

- Content editor allowing tables to be added in a consistent manner
- A system to create, manage, and track short URLs of every page on the site
- Content publishing process eliminating unnecessary steps
- A centralized system allowing curation of external content to be includ-

ed in your web properties

Regardless of the details of what functionality you are considering, that functionality needs to be carefully considered since it has the potential for such high positive impact but also additional weight / complexity to the system.

Leveraging patterns to maximize content impact

The above table is not in the least bit meant to communicate that content is not important, and certainly one piece of content can have a strong impact. That said, by searching for patterns, and applying them to lots of content, the content can have even higher impact. For example, instead of discussing creating one-off changes for a particular piece of content, by looking for patterns we may discover a method that improves all subsequent content (for example, instead of creating a nice data table for one piece of content there may be a way of enabling this data output for all content). Also, over time adding ineffective content can have a very bad impact on a site, so also see "Content publishing" in the section on streamlining common activities in Part 3.

We need to make sure to get these high-impact items, from key functionality to the templating approach, right in the first place, especially those that add weight to the system. Two ways we have leverage in creating this high impact is in architecting standards and requirements engagement, which we'll look at next.

The standards conundrum

Standards. The word probably causes some readers' skin to crawl. But if we are looking broadly at our website, then we have to face the issue of standards. As this chapter will show, standards are a bit more subtle than are perhaps obvious at first, and the product manager is a key factor when it comes to standards in two ways: 1) any request has the opportunity to break a standard (and that is usually the easiest to implement as well) and 2) for those elements that everyone agrees should be standardized, there are a lot of opportunities to streamline things in such a way that everyone wins.

> The enemy of art is the absence of limitations. — Orson Welles

Flexibility: get focused

As Seth Gottlieb wrote in an excellent blog post, "Flexibility. It's a matter of perspective,"[11] there are many different meanings of "flexible" among content creators, web designers, print designers, and developers. I would add another key stakeholder: the overall web presence owner who may want branding consistency. Put even more broadly, the website needs to be 1) coherent and 2) able to make site-wide changes.

Inflexibility in two steps, starting with... flexibility

The interesting thing about flexibility is that on the small scale it is trivial. This is one of the biggest problems, since it is tough to argue with stakeholders who are reminding us how easy it is to implement what they are asking for ("I did this on my iPad while we were talking – this is obviously easy!"). So when push comes to shove, especially in the heat of making lots of big changes to a website, we let stakeholders do whatever it takes to implement whatever they think is necessary. For example, we might open up the WYSIWYG editor to allow any HTML, or we might let one group launch a microsite on another platform. In other words, we may start with flexibility. But then later the inflexibility settles in. What happens when we want to

---

11 http:/contenthere.net/2013/06/flexibility-its-a-matter-of-perspective.html

change the way all the data tables look across the site? Oops, that's now hard since the data is implemented in an inconsistent manner. What about when someone wants to change teams in the organization? They now may have to learn different tools. We all know cases where even getting the logo the same across the web presence is difficult.

The flexibility dynamic

There are two sides to the flexibility equation: 1) immediate flexibility and 2) long-term flexibility. For example, when someone is publishing a page that needs to include a data table with special features, then they want – now – the flexibility to make that happen. This may fly in the face of long-term flexibility when it comes to standardizing how data tables work (perhaps also allowing additional features where all data tables have manipulation or download tools).

Streamlining and product management over time

In many ways immediate flexibility and long-term flexibility aren't as in conflict as they appear, since almost always everyone wants to work faster. In digging deeper, usually there are known common publishing (or site management) needs that should be streamlined. Lots of people complaining about needing to control their left nav item? Instead of just letting people completely control their section's left nav, perhaps by talking with the stakeholders you realize that really all that is needed is the ability to add one custom link. Of course, the details of your website are unique, but usually if you go a little deeper in investigating issues you can find a lot more commonality than is immediately obvious. On an ongoing basis, you should be product managing your website for ongoing quality, change, and coherence, including defining your ongoing work program. Looking for opportunities to streamline things for stakeholders, while offering an appropriate level of flexibility, is an important piece of product management. See "Streamline common activities" in Part 3.

Making big changes? Focus to help frame the flexibility discussion.

For teams doing early planning in developing master plans, one of the most important aspects is clearly defining the vision of what they are attempting. This probably includes refining the vision: as teams dive into the different aspects of their vision (and at a high level the people, processes, technology, content, etc. required to implement it) to confirm that it will work, they will probably realize the vision needs to change a bit.

This process of defining the vision while confirming it is possible is important when defining flexibility for the following reasons:

- It grounds the discussion of control, both initially and on an ongoing basis (and having these discussions early rather than later means fewer blow-ups down the line).
- Senior management has an opportunity to confirm or change the broad goals, rather than jumping right into details (where different stakeholders may push for flexibility that runs counter to broader goals). Note that with one recent client of mine, it became obvious that senior management (as opposed to particular site owners) was very interested in consistency and being able to make web presence–wide changes, so this could be accounted for in the vision and master plan.

Flexibility in grayscale

Content contributors often hear the word "standards" and run for the hills, and people often think in terms of flexibility in a binary "yes, flexible" or "no, locked down" way.

How flexibility vs. standards might feel

But it's much more subtle than this, and will probably be the topic of another blog post. That said, here are some key things to look at when defining how flexible to make your site:

- What sites (if you have a large web presence with lots of sites or sections of sites) will be standardized and which ones will be completely on their own?
- What components of pages / IA will be standardized? For example, a standard template could be nothing more than a shell with a standard header and footer, or it could prescribe many more components on a page.
- How deep will the standards be? For a particular component that is being standardized, is it completely locked down to a particular value, a palette of options, open with some filtering, or completely open?

In other words, flexibility is more in grayscale than black and white, and you should attempt to shoot for the middle ground, allowing streamlined flexibility.

Try to think of and implement flexibility as more nuanced.

53

These issues will be expanded below.

Standards pervasiveness

You may envision a website that is managed with military precision, but what does your site visitor see? With more and more site visitors entering your site at arbitrary (and perhaps even forgotten) pages, chances are that they are seeing a lot of inconsistency rather than consistency. But how consistent is your site? Let's explore this before discussing how to pull off a consistent website.

> The nice thing about standards is there are so many to choose from. — Andrew Tanenbaum

Let's start with what I feel should be the most basic measure of consistency: the percentage of pages that meet a particular standard (or perhaps "all" your standards). Let's take the example of having a standard logo, header, footer, and styling for the left nav across your site. If your site is 10,000 pages and only 1,000 use the standard logo, header, footer, and styling, then you only have 10% consistency on that standard. In other words, you should be evaluating results and not whether you have some standards written out in some crusty standards document somewhere. The point here isn't even that you necessarily are highly accurate in measuring your standardization, but that you are being focused on your actual web pages (since, again, your website visitors may not even go to your primary pages).

When looking at any standard, consider how pervasive that standard is. The following pervasiveness scale can help you figure out where you are on your standards (use the table to evaluate each standard and not your standards en masse):

Standards Pervasiveness Scale	
1. Obscured	There may be some incidental consistency, but this element hasn't been standardized meaningfully.
2. Suggested	Something that the team is considering standardizing upon.
3. Planned	You have plans to standardize this.

4. Defined	The standard is defined.
5. Implemented	The standard is implemented in at least one central system rendering some relevant pages.
6. Consistent	The standard is implemented across the web presence.

Before declaring you have instituted a new standard, consider how pervasive it is.

Some particular things to watch out for:

- "Build it and they will come" mentality. This happens when perhaps a key central system (maybe even the official one that everyone is supposed to use) may have many standards built into it, but a vast majority of pages are not even rendered by this system. In other words, this is a standard that is stuck at level 5 above.
- "The standard is defined" trap. If you have defined a standard in some static document, then chances are many people don't even know about it. This would be a standard that hasn't gone past level 4.
- Standards that, in an attempt to be broad, actually obscure important standards. For example, if you only have defined standards at a low level (like perhaps what HTML tags are acceptable) then you may be overlooking standards for particular types of content (like not standardizing how events look). This would be a standard at the Obscured level.

Standards aren't defined — they're architected.

It seems to me that many times style guides or other standards are written without much thought about how they will get implemented. In my opinion, standards should be architected and not simply defined. In fact, I would go further and say that a standard shouldn't even be defined if you haven't figured out a way of implementing it.

As a way of grounding your discussion of standards, you could start with an inventory of the pervasiveness of your standards. For instance, how many of your standards are defined? How many of those are only implemented for a portion of your site? How many are consistent across your entire web presence?

Let's assume you find some standards that aren't yet consistent across your entire web presence. You can then look at whether those standards are:

- Understood
- Agreed upon, and
- Easy for the content contributor or site owner to implement.

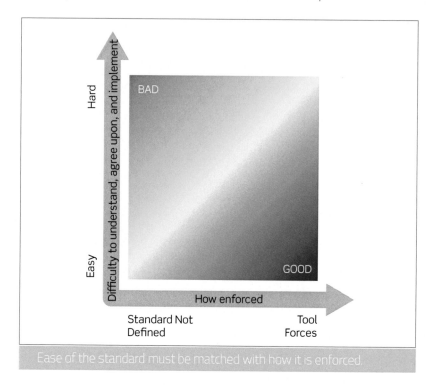

Ease of the standard must be matched with how it is enforced.

If any of these three things aren't in place, then it's easy to see why the standard is not being implemented consistently. The key is to match the ease from the content contributor's perspective with how it is implemented in the system. For instance, if you have standards around how tables are supposed to display but it is difficult for the content contributor to pull this vision off, then the tool should allow the content owner to more easily meet the standard or you have the burden of extra training.

How do you know if you've architected your standards rather than just defined them?

- Most or many of your standards have been consistently implemented across your web presence.

- You considered how easy it is to understand, agree upon, and implement the standards for content contributors, and you matched the technical implementation accordingly.
- When content contributors and site owners look at the standards, they understand what they have to actively implement themselves and which ones will be automatically handled by the system.
- It's easy to roll out new standards and changes to existing standards.
- You have considered how the templates enforce and cascade key standards.
- You have considered different levels of standards, including standards that are parameterized rather than just fixed.

Experiments

Experimentation is one of the reasons to have a regular cycle of website changes (the regular cycle is described in more detail in Ongoing Change further on in the book). That said, experimentation should be done while thinking long term and broadly about your web presence. If only one team "wins" by doing an experiment, then it isn't that useful an experiment from a website product management perspective. For example, if a new method of presenting a data table is implemented on one page then it is a useful experiment if it might (depending on the results of the experiment) be applied to other pages and site sections. If it's just something that will forever live on only one page and not be extended elsewhere then it probably is just leading to further clutter on the site (breaking your standards in the process).

Aside from pure content experiments that can be done within your standards, consider the following when experimenting:

- Implement in a way that could reasonably be extended to other pages / sections / sites.
- It does not benefit just one group.
- You have defined what you are testing.
- Implementing the experiment is considered as part of the normal ongoing change cycle.
- You have figured out how to "unwind" the experiment if it does not provide the desired results. For example, will the content go back to the way it was before the experiment? Will the content be labeled as a test?

The ways standards constrain

Perhaps the most important thing to keep in mind when thinking about standards is that having a standard doesn't mean completely locking down the user. This was already discussed in "Flexibility: get focused," but in this section we will look a bit more at the ways that standards constrain.

> A foolish consistency is the hobgoblin of small minds. — Ralph Waldo Emerson

From the most permissive to the most restrictive, here is a list of some of the ways that standards can constrain:

1. **Wide open.** In this case, the content contributor can put in whatever content they want (for example, any raw HTML they wish).
2. **Cut-and-paste library.** There is a library of widgets that is basically just a code library that content and site owners can copy and paste. These widgets can easily be broken either intentionally or by accident.
3. **Filtered / validated.** Certain aspects of the inserted code are checked and potentially filtered or changed (based on tags, accessibility, spelling, etc.).
4. **Parameterized.** Rather than just let the user put in whatever they want, there is a library of components that can be utilized by the site or content owner, which is controlled by parameters (such as a palette of acceptable colors).
5. **Fixed.** The site or content owner has no control.

The level of constraint you decide to apply has an important impact on how well your standards happen. For example, a cut-and-paste library may sound good and easy to implement, but over the long haul may erode down to pretty much wide open. In general, you should get to the highest level of constraint that will satisfy the required flexibility. In particular, parameterized is a very desirable level since it not only provides a decent level of standardization but it also makes things much easier for the user.

Where standards apply

We just covered some ways that standards constrain. Next we look at *where* they apply. Both as a means to confirm that you have sufficiently covered what needs to be standardized, but also as a means of thinking how they will be implemented, consider the following layers of standards:

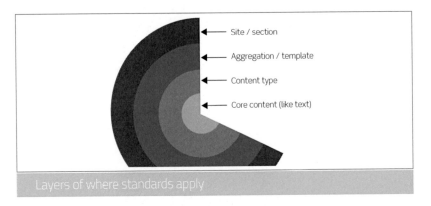

Layers of where standards apply

Breaking these layers out into more specifics, standards can be applied many places, including:

- Platform
- Template
- Information architecture (top level and site-specific)
- Functional widgets
- Editorial
- Format-specific standards
- URL and API standards
- Metadata
- Creation and management of sites
- Content workflow
- Website rollout process
- Skill levels of content publishers

When looking at achieving your business goals, consider which of these types of standards need to be defined. Don't just blindly define standards for all of them without anchoring on the business goals.

Templating and roles

Especially for large sites, defining a templating strategy as well as who controls what parts of the templating can mean a large swing in the effort of maintaining (and also rolling out) sites. In particular, there's always the question of how easy it would be to make a global change across all pages of the site. Thinking about the layers of content and templates that roll up to generate a page can help improve your ability to make global alterations like logo changes as discussed above.

As an example, consider this simple web page on the hobbsontech.com site:

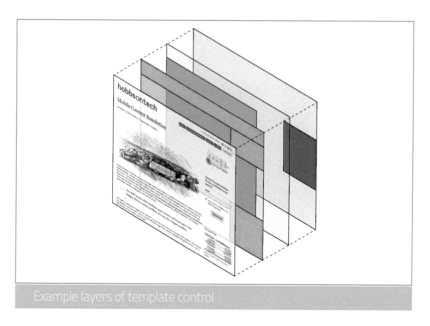

Example layers of template control

The global template controls many parts of the page, but note that some areas are only partially defined by the global template. For instance, the styling of the title of the blog post is defined but the actual title is defined by the content itself. For large sites, there may be a lot of depth in the templating, as well as roles for who controls what level.

Sites with many subsites or sections are often cumbersome to manage. This difficulty can occur even when standards have been defined, but they were implemented separately for each subsite. If the implementation was separate like that, then it may be extremely expensive to modify the standard. So in particular for large sites, consider how standards are inherited from the site hierarchy and what system should actually implement each layer.

You just read MAXIMIZE IMPACT.
Now take at least this one action:

When discussing standards and website flexibility, consider how pervasively the standards apply and whether you can implement them systematically.

Engage for better requirements

True engagement with stakeholders is an essential element of website product management, and requirements definition is a primary activity where this engagement happens. It also is an area where product management is key.

When to define requirements

The process described in Ongoing Change below means that you are always inching toward a deeper and more insightful definition of problems and their solutions.

On a routine basis, the most intense requirements definition occurs when final work program decisions are being made, to define concretely what is going to be implemented. That said, even before that the gradual definition of requirements is occurring. That's because even the stage of clarifying the request is a form of requirements definition. The point is that you never waste a huge amount of time defining absolute ideal requirements that may never be implemented, which is obviously a waste of everyone's time.

There is actually an even more intense period: when about to undertake a large transformation such as a replatforming project. A replatforming project is an important time to carefully define requirements for the site's skeleton and the backend since these aspects are going to be implemented early on anyway (whether or not they are carefully defined and understood).

Avoid big bangs

Big bang thinking still plagues our industry. This happens in many areas, with perhaps the most common being the focus on big launches rather than phasing in over time (see *Website Migration Handbook v2* for more on phasing). Look no further than Healthcare.gov as an example of a failed big bang launch. But this is just one example of Big Up-Front Requirements (see "BUFR" on the Cauvin blog) that carry many disadvantages, the largest of which is that it's difficult to know all the requirements up front. One of the reasons to structure Ongoing Change as described further in this book is to force everyone to think about what can be implemented in the near term.

Another reason to avoid big bang requirements is that embracing them fosters the development of requirements that cannot be implemented. When one team says to another to "just give us the requirements," it frequently means the requesting team spends effort defining the absolute ideal, which forces all teams to go back to the drawing board when that ideal cannot be implemented in a reasonable timeframe.

Don't "gather" requirements

Can we all agree to drop the term "requirements gathering"? Nothing could be further from the right way to do requirements than to gather them, as if they are simply scattered about and need to be brought to one list. That said, this is still how most organizations think about requirements, and the results show. By far the majority of requirements that I see organizations put together are disjointed and don't strike at the core needs of their website. Why you shouldn't just harvest requirements:

- It radically reduces the possibility of breakout and game-changing improvements.
- Many stakeholders have a very limited view of both their part of the web presence and the industry at large.
- By focusing on collection, it reduces the chance of searching for commonality.

- Most stakeholders are only concerned about their sphere of influence.
- Most discussions are in comparison to what exists now, so they are about incremental improvements.
- The requirements become disjointed and fragmented.
- Related to the above bullet, but slightly different, the requirements become unfocused (you can imagine requirements that are completely coherent / consistent, but are still so diffuse that they lose what is most important about the site).

We will come back to the best way to engage with everyone on requirements, but first let's look at what good requirements look like. Then we can get into how to get there.

Don't be afraid to surprise.

At the World Bank, I was product manager for the content publishing platform for over a thousand World Bank sites and we had a seemingly endless list of requests from the hundreds of content contributors for improvements. The list of requests always grew more than it shrank. One time, the lead developer said he had an idea to completely change the first page people saw when they logged into the CMS. But no one had asked for this. I have to admit, I was nervous about prioritizing this change over our huge backlog of requests. In the end, we went with it. Guess what? The CMS users were thrilled. It helped both power and occasional users. And no one complained that item #428 or whatever wasn't implemented to make room for this change.

There are probably lots of lessons to glean from this little story, but the one I'd like to emphasize here is that it's ok to give an unexpected response to the "requirements" that your people may lob at the central team. Sometimes it's even ok to ignore what people are saying and instead give them what they need. They might be delighted (at least for a while!) rather than everyone complaining about request numbers. Of course, this requires finesse, skill, and a bit of luck — and you can't ignore your stakeholders in general. But when getting into the decisions of what gets implemented, listening to the deeper needs of the teams is more important than literally what everyone is saying.

In the case of surprising users, we are NOT talking about "gold plating" here (where the development team adds features at the time of implementation). Rather, we are referring to a completely different response to a request than what has been specifically requested.

Keep all, deliver some.

You're not going to satisfy all of everyone's requirements. Also, some people will take your talking about or investigating possible solutions as an indication that something will get implemented. For instance, sometimes your stakeholders will ask, "We've been talking about this for years when is it going to be implemented?" The short answer: "possibly never". The difference between a request and a commitment to deliver must be very clearly delineated. One recommendation is to have a list where every unit (perhaps one person per unit can enter requests) can enter whatever requests they want. Requests would never get deleted, but it would be clear which items were not committed for delivery. If you have a voting system, then you could encourage the person who requested the feature to lobby others to vote. With voting in particular, you could clearly point to the request system, indicating that no one else voted for it. This also helps with the "this obviously is important" or "this is an institutional priority" when obviously no one is interested enough to vote. You should have the final say on what goes into the product (taking into account resources, batching features in a reasonable way, and other infrastructure needs that most stakeholders are not aware of), but voting is a solid and clear way to get important input from your stakeholders.

What good requirements look like

If you read generic books on requirements, you'll see lists of characteristics of excellent requirements like complete, correct, feasible, necessary, prioritized, unambiguous, verifiable, complete, consistent, modifiable, and traceable.[12] That said, for websites I would suggest that any requirements should have the following characteristics:

- Coherent
- Implementable in the short term
- Anchored on the business
- Clear to everyone
- Communications enhancing

Coherent. A whole section above is dedicated to the need to think broad-

12 *Software Requirements 3* by Karl Wiegers and Joy Beatty

ly and long term about your web presence. This means that your require-ments need to be coherent, especially in that they must fit within the larger context of your website (rather than simply being coherent themselves). Becoming incoherent is far easier to occur on a website than many other products since it is, on one level, so easy to make changes. So you have to always be vigilant to make sure that your requirements are coherent.

Implementable in the short term. A core theme of treating your website as a product is the need to constantly phase in improvements. This means that you always need to define requirements such that they can be imple-mented in the next phase. Sometimes larger initiatives will not fit into this cycle, but in general you should be able to define chunks that can be imple-mented within each phase.

Anchored on the business. Given the distributed nature of input and own-ership of websites, it's easy to wind up implementing things that serve the squeaky wheels rather than those that actually address a business need. The triangle of stakeholders from the beginning of this handbook should help to ensure that you are anchoring on the business (and the closest proxy for the business, the site visitors!). Fundamentally, your requirements should be able to answer "What business need does this requirement ad-dress?"

The question of whether the requirement addresses a business need isn't enough. Strong requirements also focus and isolate the business need within the broader context. For example, if a department asks for an iPhone app for customers to schedule visits with their department, then imple-menting that request would address a business need (better scheduling). But it would not be anchored on the business because:

- It does not consider whether other departments would benefit from the same thing, and, once the door is open to a department-specific app, it's hard to reel that back in.
- It doesn't consider whether an app is really the right approach at all. Perhaps just building that functionality into the website makes sense.

So a second question is: "Is this an appropriate way to address the business need?"

Clear to everyone. Talk is cheap, and there is a lot of it. It's easy to throw

65

around buzzwords like "iPhone app," "mobile," "big data," and "responsive." But without further defining exactly what it is that you will be doing to address the business need (incidentally resulting in, for example, an iPhone app), then it will be easy for different teams to expect different things. The worst outcome here is to spend a lot of time implementing something, throwing around "mobile," only to disappoint different teams that are expecting different things but using the same word.

Communications enhancing. Clarity isn't the only point for using requirements to enhance communications. Defining requirements should pull teams together. If a wide range of people are interested in creating SEO-targeted landing pages, then those people should get together to discuss what is important. So requirements can pull teams together.

Note in particular that you should NOT attempt to be complete in your requirements definition. The primary reason is that in attempting to be thorough it is very easy to miss the entire point of whatever you are trying to implement. In addition, a major issue is that it reduces the chance to get quicker feedback.

Stakeholder engagement for requirements

The process outlined in "Always phase improvements" greatly ameliorates stakeholder engagement since it sets up a process for constantly working with stakeholders to better the website. Also, streamlining common flows (from chapter 6) means that less time is wasted discussing the common tasks. Note that one of the advantages of having constant phasing of new changes is that it encourages everyone to think creatively about how to create valuable changes in the short term (the next phase). That said, the requirements definition process is usually pretty ineffective. Next we'll look at common problems and a better way of engaging for requirements:

Bad and better engagement	
Common (bad) practice	**Better practice**
Lobbing requirements / using requirements as a weapon	Collaborating
Endless talking	Focused discussions

Big bang requirements	Incremental requirements
Not involving important stake-holders in the requirements	Effective involvement of import-ant stakeholders
Some of the most common patterns are ineffective.	

Collaborate instead of using requirements as a weapon.

Having spent much of my professional life on the technical side of the world, I'm amazed at how often this statement arises: "They haven't told us the full requirements. Once the business users give us the requirements, we can get back to them with the level of effort."

Are you on the technical team? Before uttering the above words, first consider whether you are missing an important opportunity to shape the requirements. Are you on another team? Try to use the points here to encourage more of a dialogue with developers.

Obviously the word "requirements" is not ideal in the first place. Some people get hung up on "a requirement is a requirement", but requirements are more subtle than that. By slightly shifting assumptions, you can often satisfy the underlying need with different written requirements. For example, I might say, "I need to receive an email when a user signs up for our newsletter". But what if I got the response "Since we already all carry cellphones, and we have such a specialized newsletter that signups are rare, could we send it as a text instead — also, you might not be aware that we're having problems with our email notification system so we would rather avoid adding functionality to it"? I might say, sure that's fine. So if I stuck to the requirement as originally stated it might take a long time and lead to greater instability, but by talking about it we wound up with a reasonable (perhaps better) solution that is more stable. Yes, if you're a stickler then you might say that the true requirement was notification and not email or text specifically, but the point is that talking about the requirements is more effective than lobbing written documents at each other. Obviously, this was a trivial example, but your requirements probably are not trivial so the ante is higher in moving toward strong requirements.

Why are teams tempted to use the give-us-the-full-requirements-first approach? Some possible reasons:

- Business users often do not understand their own requirements, and technical teams have been burned with shifting requirements once development starts.

- Being overwhelmed with requests, this maneuver helps ensure that the business group is serious about these requirements.
- If the work will be farmed out by the technical team, having very clear up-front requirements will help in that process.
- Pure defensiveness ("covering" yourself in the event that things go wrong), especially if relations between technical and other teams have significantly broken down.

What are the problems of shifting the burden to the business side? A few main issues:

- Extended time period from initial idea to implementation
- Limited opportunity to define ideal solution
- Increases adversarial relationship

The first two issues above arise since there could be a very wide gap between the expectations of the business users and what can be implemented. Let's say the business users are imagining a castle, and write a huge document laying out the castle requirements including a moat. The technical team sees this and all they can work with is leather and wood, so they suggest a teepee with a pond. Obviously, if this is the start of the "negotiations" then it's going to be a long discussion (especially if the teams just lob documents at each other). Let's say that you eventually end up with a reasonable brick house (perhaps the masons on the tech team became available). Another subtle issue that arises in this type of arrangement: the business team still remembers that they wanted a castle and will compare the end result to the castle. The technical team will remember they first wanted to do a teepee and think anything more sophisticated than that is a favor. So the expectations really did not start things off on a good footing.

So what is a better approach? Collaborating from the start. From the technical perspective, you have the opportunity to shape the requirements in a useful direction. Some specific recommendations:

- When first discussing requirements, always make it clear what elements of the request are easy and which ones are difficult. Moreover, consider how, if the requirement changed slightly and the approach was a bit different, it would be far easier and more reliable to implement. In addition, the business team should consider the impacts to them if the functionality is implemented (for instance, the need for a community manager to drive a new forum).

- Have a process for product managing these change requests (including deciding what gets implemented and what does not), and have product management take the lead on bringing the teams together to deliver a high-quality and consistent implementation.
- Don't implement anything that will cause significant degradation of overall quality or reliability.
- Document the pros/cons of implementing the request and the process leading to your decision on it.

Agile methodologies help encourage a more collaborative approach, but regardless of the methodology you use, consider working with the business users in developing your requirements.

Focus instead of endless talking

One very common but unproductive route that companies take is extensive and unfocused stakeholder interviews. Requirements discussions should be structured and not completely open ended. For example, first the vision should be defined, and then you can dive into the further details with those who are particularly concerned about that functionality. This is much more difficult in practice of course. Here are some quick suggestions for more productive discussions:

- Anchor all discussions on the vision.
- Provide some type of penalty for not being involved in requirements discussions when invited and then later complaining about the outcome.
- Attempt to focus more on what the desired outcome is than the current details of the problem.
- Don't make promises until a change is committed to in the work program.
- Inch toward the requirements (don't waste time detailing something that won't get implemented — sounds obvious but this happens all the time).

Who are the relevant stakeholders?

Some readers may recoil at the term "stakeholder" since it sounds a bit abstract and bureaucratic. But the point is that as the website product manager you need to talk with everyone who is impacted by the website, the backend, or the outcomes of the website. Yes, that's everyone who holds a stake in the website, and it's a lot of people. As we already discussed, good engagement isn't about endless talking, so you don't need to talk to everyone all the time. That said, here are some of the stakeholders of a website:

Stakeholders		
Type	**Stakeholders**	**Type of feedback**
Business owners	• CEO / CxO • Website owner • Product manager	Critical information on the business need of the website
Site visitors (external)	Audience segmentation depends on your company — also "Long-term engagement funnels" in Part 1	How the website needs to behave and look (to meet the business need)
Backend users (internal)	How you define these individuals depends on your workflow and environment, but includes: • Casual contributors • Power users • Group administrators	How the tools need to work
Implementation team	• DBAs • System administrators • Developers • Project managers • Liaisons and coordinators	How easy it will be to implement and maintain
Support team	• Helpdesk • Trainers	What are common issues that arise that should be handled better by the product
Content owners	• Subject matter experts (on the content) • Division heads and managers	How the website needs to behave in order to best present these individuals' expertise
Make sure you get input from all the relevant stakeholders.		

71

Note that division heads are not listed under business owners, since they often have narrow views on the needs of the site.

The point isn't to make sure you go through and talk with all these people whenever you are gathering requirements. The aim is to simply consider whether their perspectives are being included if relevant.

You just read ENGAGE FOR BETTER REQUIREMENTS.
Now take at least this one action:

Drop the term "requirements gathering" and instead start *defining* requirements.

Summary of Part 2: Getting the Bones Right

- Instead of concentrating on launches (and relaunches), concentrate on getting the bones right and then iterating from there.
- Your CMS probably isn't the problem. More specifically, your CMS may be a problem now, but without focusing you will probably wind up in the same place on a new CMS.
- Work to **maximize impact** when you make changes.
- Carefully architect your standards (instead of just defining them).
- Collaborate and engage with stakeholders to define and evolve requirements.

Part 3
Ongoing change

Even if you are thinking long term and broadly, to effectively move forward on your web presence you need to always make changes. By streamlining those changes that need to happen quickly, and committing to constantly evaluating and rolling out bigger changes, you can handle change more effectively.

> Life is like riding a bicycle. To keep your balance you must keep moving. — Albert Einstein

Some website changes should happen quickly. Others should happen slowly. Some changes shouldn't happen at all.

Routine creation of content, assuming the content pushes the business goals forward, should be simple to quickly publish. But many requests are for one-offs. These requests have a higher cost and should be considered together to find patterns that can help the site overall.

Consider the diagram below, where there are two tasks that are streamlined: creating new sites (that meet stringent standards) and new content. New content, assuming it is of reasonable quality and appropriateness, should be easy to do quickly. If the content for some reason is difficult to implement (perhaps adding advanced functionality), then it does not happen quickly and goes into the suggestion box. Similarly, perhaps there are some types of sites that are standardized, with a consistent implementation and minimum standards. Instances of these should also be implemented quickly, but only if they meet stringent standards. Those items that go into the suggestion box aren't forgotten, with a regular phasing over time to review and discuss requests.

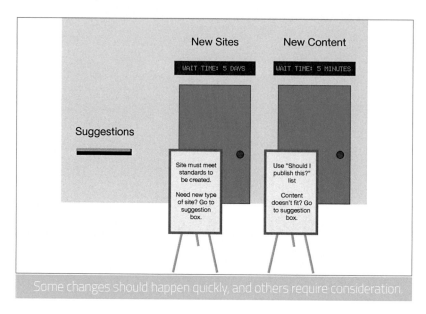

New Sites   New Content

WAIT TIME: 5 DAYS   WAIT TIME: 5 MINUTES

Suggestions

Site must meet standards to be created.

Need new type of site? Go to suggestion box.

Use "Should I publish this?" list

Content doesn't fit? Go to suggestion box.

Some changes should happen quickly, and others require consideration.

Managing the website change fire hose

Complex web presences face a nonstop flow of potential changes, from the minute-by-minute (for instance publishing content at a news organization) to the day-by-day (changing banner ads) to the month-by-month (adding new features to the site) to the year-by-year (longer range initiatives). Add to that the complication that everyone can download and implement tools on their own, so the overall expectation is that changes happen quickly.

The issue is that adding things to your website also complicates it. Organizations must make decisions on their website, all the time.

Website change boils down to three types:

1. Changes that should happen quickly, easily, and consistently (publishing everyday, essential content).
2. Changes that improve the website broadly and long term (improving the publishing process).

3. One-offs (launching a new microsite that would have served the organization better as a more integrated element of the web presence).

In general, organizations rush to implement one-offs and declare victory, even when the one-off digs them further into their current problems This often occurs since organizations are buried with urgent requests, overlooking the important underlying needs. This handbook attempts to lay a framework to rise above the fray and make the important changes.

Three types of change		
	Ability to undo, maintain, or change	**Business impact**
Quick, Easy, and Consistent (example: publishing a routine, daily update)	High	High
Broad and Long term (example: functionality used across the board)	High	Medium
One-off (examples: a one-off site, or an exception for one piece of content)	Low	Low
Avoid one-offs, and attempt to streamline frequent changes.		

If your content publishing is too onerous (or is done inconsistently), then content publishing should be improved. See "Streamline common activities" below for more information on streamlining this and other common changes. Note: obviously part of the equation is to set standards for content publishing (or whatever routine changes you make to your site), so that you aren't just optimizing publishing low quality.

Some changes need to be carefully considered and not rushed into. For example, if one team is considering email notifications for content updates, then there may be opportunities (and interest) across the organization in these features. Furthermore, the request may actually be better addressed in a fashion than how it was requested (perhaps social media notifications would be more effective). In other words, you should take the time to at least consider whether the request should be implemented in a way with broad and long-term considerations. Or if it should be done in as a one-off (or not at all).

Website product management attempts to make the biggest business impact when making changes. This means that the primary discussions for the website product manager are on *features* (or other structural changes such as global templates) since these results in the widest and deepest impact on the website.

Underlying all the recommendations in this handbook is the need to rise above the churn of requests, trends, and underlying needs so that the important changes are made.

Make changes at the right speed

What *should* happen quickly isn't the same thing as what *can* be implemented quickly. Change that is routine and standardized should be fast — for example, publishing a routine webpage update should happen quickly. But other changes should be more considered. If someone is requesting raw HTML access to their page so they can add a new feature (perhaps to use a new javascript library), then that exception is probably easy to provide. But when thinking of your web presence as a product, allowing that workaround is usually not ideal. Obviously others won't benefit by this one-off, but in addition it will always be a separate page that has to be considered separately. For example, what happens if the custom work hard-codes your current color scheme? If you need to change that across the board later, then you have it embedded in this one-off code.

Looking back up at our previous table, it could be that things that should happen quickly are taking a long time and that you are quickly creating one-offs. This may mean that you can't make long-term and broad changes (with all that churn on those things that should be happening quickly and things that shouldn't be happening at all).

As a baseline, we should be routinely considering changes that aren't currently streamlined. This is covered in "Always phase changes" below, and represents the suggestion box in the illustration at the start of this chapter. We want breathing room, and a slowness, to consider these changes.

Chances are you have some routine activities that should be streamlined. This is covered in Streamline Common Activities.

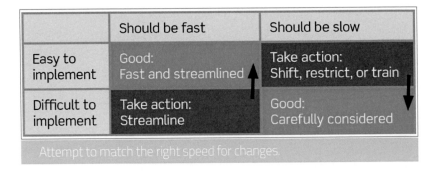

	Should be fast	Should be slow
Easy to implement	Good: Fast and streamlined	Take action: Shift, restrict, or train
Difficult to implement	Take action: Streamline	Good: Carefully considered

Attempt to match the right speed for changes.

Always phase changes

Part of getting out of the redesign-forget-redesign rut is committing to on-going change. Below I recommend a specific approach to phasing changes:

- Have a regularly scheduled process to phase in bigger website changes. For those of you doing agile development, this planning horizon needs to be longer than individual sprints.
- Post the work program so that everyone internally can see it, and also publicly post how well you deliver against that work program.
- Look beyond just popularity (or loudness of the requester) of requests for change.
- Only plan the next phase, and go beyond "yes" and "no" responses to requests.

We'll look at each of these in more detail below, but let's start with some reasons that ongoing website changes don't happen.

Enemies of ongoing website transformation

For all the talk about not wanting to do big bang redesigns, that's still pretty much what we all do. I've done my share of down-to-the-minute, global, big bang launches when they were necessary. But for now let's all agree that ongoing changes are preferable. Why do we keep doing big redesigns?

The pursuit of the shiny. Some Big Thinker inside the organization or out-side defines some shiny and immensely desirable vision for the new site, and this is often more an emotional appeal than anything else. But every-one knows implementing this vision would mean a Big Change. There's no way around it! We're just going to roll up our sleeves and get it done. Now, often you'll be aiming for a castle with a moat but get a teepee with a pud-dle by the time you launch, but conceptually everyone desires this ambi-tious vision and throws themselves at the task (or perhaps over the cliff).

 Incentives to plant flags. Let's face it: most everyone wants to Get It Done in order to claim victory. System integrators want to complete their state-ment of work, get paid, and slap another client logo on their site. VPs want to claim victory. Everyone just wants to move on from what's perceived as a painful task (which is more painful when big bang).

Ease of understanding. Anyone can look at the current site and see the problems. And everyone thinks they understand (again, at least emotion-ally) where they want to go. But even if they don't completely understand where you're headed, one thing is for sure: one day it will be like it is now, and another it will be improved. Nice and tidy to understand (again, at least it seems that way at the beginning).

Pent-up demand. Often as a result of the big bang mentality, a website gets little attention in between redesigns. That means after the hacked-to-gether system is no longer viable, there is such a pent-up demand that it's hard to phase in changes. By always phasing improvements, although it will never result in all requested items being implemented, the pent-up demand will be reduced (especially the urgent needs).

Handoffs. Almost always, the approach goes something like this: 1) Tell us (tech team) what you (site owner) want. 2) We tell you what you'll get. 3) Find out midstream you can't get there. 4) Deliver less than step 2. This is because the details of how to get there aren't thought about in design. But the mere thought that this handoff occurs back and forth means that there's an incentive for these issues to happen less frequently. Refer back to "Engage for better requirements" in Part 2 for more on reducing handoffs.

Need to demonstrate something. Sometimes what is needed is purely backend, like better content management. But sometimes organizations feel that more needs to be demonstrated, so before we know it the project is even more complex than it needs to be.

Regular, planned phases of improvements

An anchor of website product management is frequent, planned phases of improvements. This planning provides a structure for the constant barrage of potential changes you could make to your site, in order to target those that have the highest impact for your business. At its core, what's needed is straightforward, but in practice there is a lot of finesse involved. Here are the main components of a useful website work program:

1. Only the next phase is planned.
2. The schedule for phasing steps (for example, when will the next phase be defined) is known far in advance (but not exactly what will be implemented in future phases).

Very short cycles don't count

One of the goals of this handbook is to help you dig out of floundering in urgent tasks. If you have weekly or bi-weekly meetings to discuss what is imminently getting implemented, you won't have much time to breathe to think big nor will you have the time to get input from a wide range of stakeholders on that cycle. Having very short cycles of development makes sense, but if you do that you also need longer phases as well. This section is talking about longer phases, using three months as an example .

Ongoing cycle

At a top level, you have a recurring cycle of three steps:

1. **Define.** The functionality changes for the next short duration (say three months). At this point, you would define what will be implemented in the next phase, and what the success criteria would be for that phase.
2. **Implement.** Implement what you defined for this three-month cy-

cle. Preferably even this phase would be conducted in an iterative fashion so that you have the chance to react as the phase is being implemented versus potentially being surprised later on.

3. **Review.** Review the following three aspects after your implementation: a) how this phase performed against the success criteria you set at the beginning, b) your previously planned steps for this phase, and c) other requests that have come up since your last review.

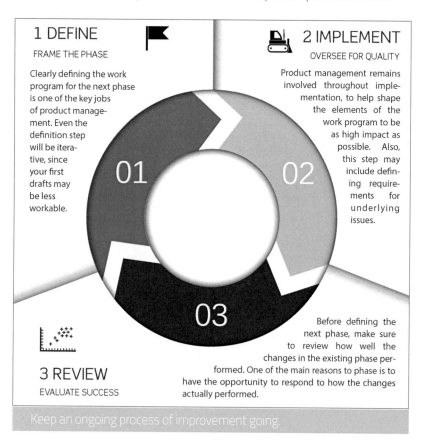

1 DEFINE

FRAME THE PHASE

Clearly defining the work program for the next phase is one of the key jobs of product management. Even the definition step will be iterative, since your first drafts may be less workable.

01

2 IMPLEMENT

OVERSEE FOR QUALITY

Product management remains involved throughout implementation, to help shape the elements of the work program to be as high impact as possible. Also, this step may include defining requirements for underlying issues.

02

03

3 REVIEW

EVALUATE SUCCESS

Before defining the next phase, make sure to review how well the changes in the existing phase performed. One of the main reasons to phase is to have the opportunity to respond to how the changes actually performed.

Keep an ongoing process of improvement going.

In practice, these steps overlap. For instance, for a large organization you may have requests coming into a formal change request tracking system all the time. But you may only process them at a particular time. This approach helps to elevate wider problems to patterns rather than solely responding to individual requests.

There are several key reasons to phase in this manner:

- Faster to see new functionality / pages on the new CMS
- Sets the stage for continuous improvement of the web presence
- Better ability to react to changes
- Less time specifying what needs to be done at each stage

Example: detailed engagement steps

As mentioned above, although exactly what will be implemented is only defined for the next cycle, the schedule is known well in advance. To illustrate this, consider that the work program is defined something like this:

Example: Work program for January–March	
Making our site more actionable	<ul><li>For each template, define a default call to action (to be used if not overridden by the specific page).</li><li>Start training on making the site more actionable.</li></ul>
Streamlining publishing	<ul><li>By default drop the preview step for publishing content.</li><li>Reduce the number of fields required for publishing the product pages.</li><li>Disallow custom formatting by default.</li></ul>
Various	<ul><li>Add new Bio content type (migration of content items to be manual by content owners).</li><li>Fix Chrome crashing in the custom data display widget (bug #281473).</li></ul>

An example of the work program for website changes in the current quarter

In this case, nothing is committed to beyond March. You can imagine that there is a huge list of other requests that are not on this list. You don't want to leave your stakeholders high and dry on these requests. This is where the schedule for making decisions is known far in advance. Although the details of your schedule would depend on your organization, consider this representative ongoing cycle:

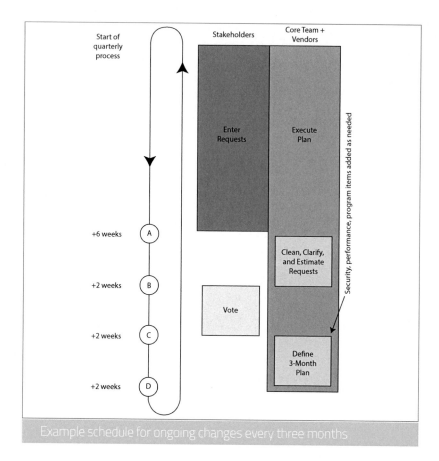

Example schedule for ongoing changes every three months

In our example, the defined work program starts on January 1st ("Start of quarterly process" in the diagram). This means that the stakeholders can expect the following:

- The core team and vendors will be working on the January–March work program starting January 1st.
- Stakeholders can continue entering requests until February 15th (to be considered in the April–June work program).
- The core team may be request the other stakeholders for clarifications from February 15th to February 28th.
- The core team will provide a high-level estimate of effort by February 28th (perhaps a simple "high," "medium," "low" effort level designation).

- Stakeholders will vote on what items they think are most important until March 15th.
- The April-June work program will be published by March 30th.

Furthermore, everyone knows that this will always be the schedule, so everyone can bank on this fact on an ongoing basis. Engagement will be covered more in the "Requirements and engagement" chapter. For now, we will continue on the need for phasing at all, and how to define what goes into each phase.

Possible responses to requests

When deciding what to add to the work program, the possible responses to any request aren't just "yes" or "no" — in fact, these should only be used rarely. As will be discussed in "Requirements and engagement," one of the goals of website product management is to deepen engagement of everyone that has a stake in the website. Stakeholders firing off requirements with binary responses of whether they will be implemented does not help this. The following table highlights responses you should commonly use, as well as those that are a bit more dangerous so should be used more sparingly.

Table of possible responses to requests	
Solid responses	**When to use**
Yes, with shifted requirements Example: request for API to specific dataset, but instead commit to org-wide API framework (perhaps in the next three months defining the problem)	• When other stakeholders have similar needs • When original request states a solution rather than the business need

Yes, but less than requested Example: request for the ability to have any color text for a call-out box, but instead deliver a palette of colors	▪ Test hypotheses before fuller implementation ▪ Confirm stakeholder commitment (will they actually promote and use what is implemented?) ▪ Provide 80% of the value for 20% of the cost
Not now, but maybe later Example: any request that is kept in the request list but is not included in the next work program	▪ When a request does not become a priority based on the "Factors in deciding on the work program"
Occasional responses	**When to use**
No Example: request for a site that does not pass your decency standards	▪ Only when a request is radically off-base (since we don't know what the future holds, or how a better understanding of the requirements will change over time)
Yes (literally as requested) Example: fix a long-standing and clearly-understood bug in the caching process	▪ When the request is a blatant bug with a clear desired outcome ▪ Otherwise when the request is either a) extremely straightforward or b) well thought out and a clear business priority
Provide something not specifically requested Example: improve repository search (searching content in the backend) in order to improve the overall experience even though it is not specifically requested	▪ When product management sees an opportunity to radically improve the website or the backend, based on overall trends of problems or opportunities rather than responding to a specific request
Bias toward the top three responses	

Defining the work program

Through whatever steps you define, at some point you need to define what is going to be in your upcoming, short-term work program.

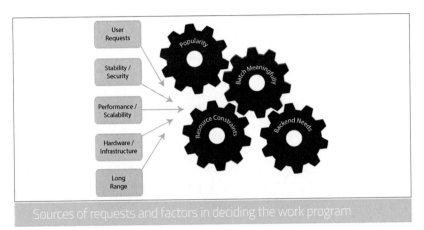

Sources of requests and factors in deciding the work program

Sources of requests

There are several streams where potential features could get added to the system:

- User requests (either internal or external)
- Stability / security
- Performance / scalability
- Hardware / infrastructure
- Long-range requirements

So even an important user request may not make it onto your near-term work program if, for example, there is a severe stability issue that needs to be addressed quickly. So there is something of an air gap between the requests coming in and what winds up on the work program. This is one of the most important roles of the product manager, and the product manager needs to consider the following factors. Note in particular that user requests as inputs may result in changes to the system that are very different from the original request.

Factors in deciding the work program

There are two parts involved in defining the work program: 1) deciding which requests you will respond to, and 2) determining how you will respond to those requests. In this section we look at the first: deciding which requests you respond to. Phasing is more of an art than a science, but here are some principles to keep in mind when phasing your requirements for initial and ongoing implementation (starting with those in the cogs in the diagram above). Note that sometimes it is necessary to define a possible approach in some detail before deciding whether or not to include it in a work program.

Backend needs. As mentioned above, key security, scalability, performance, or manageability issues may trump any other requests. Notably, these may be items that your key stakeholders may not be aware of, much less actually requesting them.

Batching. Your near-term work program needs to be consistent, meaningfully grouping changes. This is both for communications and technical reasons. From a communications perspective, if the items being addressed are consistent then everyone can quickly understand what's happening. From a technical perspective, if you need to completely rewrite a subsystem to address an issue then it might make sense to address many of the issues with that subsystem at once.

Resource constraints. Obviously you need to have the resources to implement your work program. This is for both a raw number of hours as well as balancing key resources. For instance, if your DBA is required for many requests then you may be able to only do some DBA-limited requests at once.

Popularity. Of course, the popularity of a request is very important, but, again, not the only factor. All other factors being equal, a more popular item should be placed on the work program before others. In practice, it may make sense to delay your top-requested feature in order to address the next three (for instance if the next three could be implemented in the same effort as the first).

Impact of Failure. Some items may not be urgent, or even the highest priority, but their failure should be known as early as possible. For example, you may think that something is a good idea but want to test its validity before investing deeply in it. Another example would be where the whole reason to undertake a new direction on your website is a risky area. If that's the case, then it should be tested as early as possible to maximize the chance of success.

Urgency. How urgent is the functionality needed? Is this not even needed if implemented later?

Technical Debt. In general, things should be developed in a way that won't require redoing work in the future (or in a way that future development is not boxed in or impossible). Forking code should always be avoided if possible.

Dependencies. Obviously, if one piece of functionality needs to be complete before another will work, then that forces the order. Note that this is a little more subtle than may be initially obvious: sometimes you only need to do part of a piece of functionality before another can start to be developed. Another element of dependencies is whether moving forward on something will mean rework later. For instance, you could either wait to implement something fully or start by making content changes now. These content changes may have to be undone in the future when the full technology is implemented (for example if the content changes now will be implemented in templates later).

Business priority. In the grand scheme of things, how important is this functionality? Although other factors may trump priority, the priority of a task can reasonably push its development earlier.

Effort. When taking all of the other above factors into account, you want to have the highest impact with the least effort. Note that just because a task is simple does not mean it should be implemented.

Two non-factors. Note two factors that are NOT listed as factors:

- A group being willing to pay for certain functionality (see "Groups willing to pay for their features" in Part 1)
- The length of time that an issue has been discussed

In the end, the product manager must be able to justify the work program to the stakeholders. Although clearly more of an art than a science, the factors (and ignoring the non-factors) should help in forming that solid work program.

How much impact would this change have?

One lens you must always use when considering a change is "how much impact would this change have?" Impact of course can be both negative (high additional maintenance cost with low benefit) and positive (where a large portion of the site is raised in quality with low cost). When thinking about impact, ask yourself these questions:

- What percentage of the total web presence does this affect?
- What percentage of key audiences would this affect?
- Will this move you toward business goals?
- How much weight and complexity are you adding?
- Will this make it easier to make site-wide changes, or harder?
- Is this just a shortcut or workaround, or is it striking at the heart of the problem?

Use these questions to evaluate not just whether to make a change, but how to do so. For example, you may be thinking of making a one-off change that will only take slightly more effort to have a broader impact.

Posting the work program

Pushing through ongoing changes on a website can be tough, whether it's because of inertia, other priorities, politics, or other reasons. Although there is no single magic potion, one thing can help, and that's prominently posting your near-term work program. Basically this would be listing out your upcoming work program, stating what you will be implementing when. This could be on your intranet, in an email newsletter, on the main CMS login screen, or some other place that all internal stakeholders could easily see.

Below are some of the advantages of boldly posting your work program on the wall.

Better engagement. As soon as you post what you plan on doing over the next few months, people are sure to provide their feedback. Since this feedback will probably be less coordinated at first than it will be as you improve your processes, you probably will want to start with items that you are very confident in fixing and that have wide support. At any rate, you will increase engagement by clearly indicating what you plan on doing (and hence what will not be done as well).

More reasonable work program. By publicly posting the work program, everyone will hold you accountable for it. This is good all around, but specifically it will naturally force you to suggest a work program you are confident in. Also, since everyone will see the breadth of what you are doing (rather than simply the potentially small sliver that they are concerned about), all stakeholders will better understand why all of their requests may not be possible to resolve.

Better clarity. Also, you will need to be much more clear about exactly what it is you are saying you will do. Vagueness will burn everyone but especially the owner of the work program. People may think your "fix UI" meant far more than what you meant!

Higher confidence. Even if you end up not delivering 100%, the stakeholders will respect that you stood up to say what you were going to do, and then stood up again to update them on what you did and did not accomplish. Of course, the highest confidence will be attained by consistently delivering on your promises, which then will also have the effect of less complaints on an ongoing basis.

More focus. It's easy to be vague when having distributed conversations with a wide range of stakeholders. But when you publicly state what you are doing, it will both force the person defining the work program to be more focused and also focus all the stakeholders on the near-term objectives.

This is something that can be done by even the smallest team, but it is also highly relevant for large organizations.

Implementation tracks

When developing and communicating the work program, communicating the work in implementation tracks can help to ensure you cover important work and more quickly illustrate the work program. For example, while at the World Bank I broke the work program down into five tracks:

- Ease of publishing
- Display-side improvements (the biggest track)
- Non-web content distribution / notification
- Maintenance / performance
- Sponsored (changes paid for by a business unit)

As mentioned in "Content publishing" below, a key job of the product manager is to ensure that publishing is streamlined, and hence this was always the first track that I communicated on. Display-side improvements were changes that site visitors directly saw, and non-web content distribution and notification were areas of focus at the time. Maintenance and performance captured elements that perhaps weren't on everyone's mind but were essential nonetheless (and required communication since these items may mean more interesting changes could not be made). Remember the whole thing about not caring if people were willing to pay for changes? Well, we actually set a high threshold for some sponsored requests to get implemented. But the primary point here is that it was communicated to everyone, and it was not some back room decision that some insiders made.

For each track, we listed what improvements would be made. For each improvement, we listed:

- How popular the request was (not all popular requests were implemented, and sometimes unpopular requests were implemented, but it was all very transparent).
- How the request was being responded to — sometimes the response (to a substantial request) was that we would spend some serious time working together to define the requirements, and other times it was actual implementation.
- Status of any slips. Whenever a request from the previous work program slipped into the next one, we clearly indicated that.

> **You just read ALWAYS PHASE CHANGES.**
> **Now take at least this one action:**
>
> If you don't have a process for recurring phasing, then at least start putting out a periodic plan (perhaps for every quarter) of what you intend on implementing. Then at the end of the quarter update everyone on the progress. If you already have a process, then look carefully at the list of possible responses to the requests above, and consider refining how you respond to them.

Streamline common activities

One of the most important things to maintaining a high-quality web presence is a smooth flow of common activities. First and foremost, the content publishing process must be smooth and is covered in the next section. That said, you must always remain vigilant of other events that regularly occur, even if no one else is seeing the pattern. In particular, for large web presences there is a constant pressure to create more websites or subsites — as such, we will look in detail at this flow, which can also be used as an example for other common activities that your website faces.

> **Warning: streamlining isn't a license for garbage.**
>
> Please don't optimize publishing junk. Although streamlining is extremely important, one of the reasons this is discussed toward the end of the book is because streamlining should only be for activities that regularly occur and it should fit within the context of how standards have been architected. Furthermore, for any particular item that is being streamlined there should be very clear minimum standards for creation, and these minimum standards should be enforced.

Content publishing

Depending on the nature of your business, content publishing may occur hourly, daily, weekly, or on some other regular frequency. Regardless of the exact schedule, for content that helps to achieve your business goals, publishing should be as rapid as possible while retaining high quality.

Although it is blatantly obvious to probably anyone reading this, here are some reasons to focus on streamlining content publishing in case you need to sell the idea (or convince yourself amongst your other million priorities to focus on this activity):

- Publishing happens frequently (as opposed to other streams).
- Publishing is often done by a wide range of people.
- Publishing has high impact on the website.
- Specifically, publishing is an entry point for problems into the system — also it is an excellent entry point for improved content.
- Slowdowns in publishing are obvious to a wide range of stakeholders.
- Small changes in the publishing process can usually mean big improvements in the life of the content publishers.
- Problems in publishing are an easy reason to "bail" on the official system and use some renegade system.

The publishing process is important for any website, regardless of industry or site size. That said, the importance of the publishing process is amplified when you have more publishing (either in terms of people or frequency). In particular, if you only have a small number of content publishers then you can get away with a less-than-perfect content publishing process. But if you decide to move to more distributed content entry (desired by many organizations), then you have to pay in one of two ways: 1) improve the publishing process or 2) suffer the collateral damage (increased training, dissatisfaction, and revolt) in moving forward with the existing publishing process.

Website product management is essential in creating and sustaining a strong web publishing process. Protecting the process of publishing happens at the following points of time in the lifecycle of your web presence:

- When making big changes, for example when selecting a CMS. The everyday publishing use case should be central to any CMS selection process. Note that in their demos vendors usually want to emphasize the bells and whistles of their product, and your own team members probably want to see what the product can do for their specific (perceived) needs. In many cases, you will find that the straight-through process is actually more crooked than it seems when looking at all the what-ifs.

- When prioritizing changes during the normal phasing of improvements, always giving extra weight to streamlining the content creation process.
- In particular, adding complexity to the publishing process should be strongly de-prioritized. Sometimes complexity does indeed need to be added, but it should only be done so with a heavy heart.

Although you shouldn't use training as an excuse for a poorly designed implementation, your training needs to be especially high quality for this most common use case.

We will look at requirements definition in more detail later, but the everyday publishing use case is perhaps the most important use case to consider. It's easy to get excited about all the possibilities (in other words, complexities) of a CMS and lose focus on this important use case. In the backend you may have a million moving pieces, but the point is that your content publishers must have an easy time publishing workaday content. When defining and refining your content publishing use case, consider the following:

- Start where most publishers will start. If you are in a high-volume publishing environment, then perhaps you can assume everyone is already logged in and at the right place. Usually, though, this isn't the case, and you have to consider the log-in process up to getting to the right place for publishing the content (sometimes placing the content can take some time).
- Do not include any side-tracks, but do list the activities that will routinely occur. If a publisher always has to include an image, then include that in the process. If they rarely do, then exclude it. If you plan on restricting what styling can be applied to the text, then include that restriction. If you plan on leaving styling wide open, then that openness should be part of the use case. In other words, this isn't a one-size-fits-all use case — it needs to reflect your needs.
- Include the preview process.
- End with the content being published to the live production environment and viewed by an external site visitor. If multi-site publishing is a key part of your vision, then the content should appear on all the relevant sites.

One key to focus on is the length of time from where publishers will start (the first bullet above) to where it is published (the last bullet above). In a news environment, perhaps the whole process needs to take less than a couple minutes. In other situations, an hour may be acceptable. In all cases, you obviously want to ensure the publisher knows where they are in the process and what the next step is (not requiring consulting a manual every time they need to publish).

Should I publish this content?

Obviously, we don't want to optimize generating junk on the website. As Kristina Halvorson and Melissa Rach put it in *Content Strategy for the Web (2nd edition)*: "Generally speaking, content is more or less worthless unless it does one or both of the following: Supports a key business objective [and] Fulfills your users' needs." So there need to be standards about what changes should be made, even when everything is optimized to make the changes quickly. As much as possible, enforcing quality should be "built in" (as is discussed in the section on architecting standards above), but much of the burden is definitely on the person publishing the content. You may wish to create a "Should I be publishing this?" list, with items such as:

- Will this content contribute to organizational goals?
- Does this content matter to the typical site visitor?
- Does it meet our quality and branding standards?
- Does this need to be reviewed by an appropriate subject matter expert?
- Is this written in a style that is appropriate for the web?
- Is the content focused, both in its content and pointing toward reasonable and useful next steps?
- Am I publishing this content in the right place?
- Is the tone appropriate?
- Would publishing this content retain our site focus?

Keeping your web presence small and simple

Perhaps you are sold on the idea of being small and simple as important. As mentioned above, a theme throughout this handbook is keeping things small and simple, but now we will look at four specific things you can do to keep you site small and simple:

- Don't publish junk in the first place (covered above).

- Think about deletion when creating.
- It's not just about deleting.
- Use rules to make decisions.

Think about deletion when creating.

Most of our efforts go into cranking content out onto our websites. But sometimes old stuff on your site is a major problem as well — some examples:

- Long-expired offers still appearing on the site
- Pages focusing on topics that were hot three years ago but now just make you look outdated
- A microsite that was created when funding for a new initiative at your organization (outside the web) is now very old-looking
- Content that is just wrong (for example that has old pricing)

As the examples show, we are not always talking about deleting content, but also:

- Sites or sections
- Topics or other taxonomy values
- Offers
- Products

Fundamentally, when creating one of these items you need to think about 1) whether it is relatively permanent and, if not, 2) how you will take it down when it is no longer relevant. Obviously, there is also 0) making sure the addition even makes sense when creating it in the first place.

It's not just about deleting.

Deletion is so definitive and satisfying that it's useful to first think about it. But there are other dispositions including:

- Archive.
- Leave at lower quality, especially if older content needs to be kept but can be clearly labeled as historical content.

Although more subtle, these (and other dispositions like them) are important for keeping a simple and small site:

- These other dispositions can be steps toward full deletion, something of a full-bodied and real action taken as a warning.
- From a user perspective, these other dispositions can still result in what feels like a smaller site.
- If it is politically difficult to do a full deletion, it may be relatively easy to argue for obscuring content (since the owner will still be able to access that content).

Use rules to make decisions.

At any realistic scale, it will be impossible to make deletion rules on a case-by-case basis. The decisions need to be made based on rules, so that you are negotiating and validating the rubric rather than individual content items.

The keys to using rules are bucketing and defining key minimum-quality metrics. The bucketing is how you group items in making your decisions. For example, you might have similar rules for product background pages that are different from the downloads page. These rules need to be based on easy-to-determine metrics. For instance, you may just say that you will always archive press releases after a year. This capability could then be built into the tool so that it automatically happens. See "Advanced streamlining" below for an example with topic pages that automatically get archived based on rules.

When to streamline

Streamlining common activities should be a focus of your continuing site improvements. This may seem incredibly boring, especially with all the gee-whiz hoopla that you may feel compelled to add to your site. But if you want to allow your site to improve on an ongoing basis and maintain high quality, then you need to streamline common activities. From *The Product Manager's Desk Reference* by Steven Haines: "Also like the physician, the product manager can proactively drive more predictable, positive and repeatable results with a set of protocols that provide a standard response for at least some situations."

Content publishing has already been discussed, and is a process that should be streamlined for all websites. You may have other common requests, such as:

- Sites or subsites
- Campaign-specific landing pages or microsites
- Topical pages (for instance, to respond to news events, or a new thread of research)
- Products
- Exhibits
- Biographies
- Partnership sites
- Department sites (resist!)

You should streamline a process if:

- It happens frequently.
- Many people do it.
- It is an entry point for erosion of quality.
- It supports a business goal.
- There is a natural pattern or consistency each time.
- Your organization "owns" the problem.

On the last point, consider partnership sites (perhaps you have banded to-gether with other organizations to fund a project for a common cause). In this case, you may not own them, so you may decide that these should be handled in a one-off manner, also explicitly allowing them to be hosted elsewhere and not based on your ordinary standards.

> There is nothing so useless as doing efficiently that which should not be done at all. — Peter Drucker

One problem is that the requests almost never come for streamlining a process (except for the straight content publishing process, covered above). Requests usually ask for more flexibility. I once was defining requirements for a news room, and the original reason I was brought in was that the system they had did not support enough design flexibility. After listening to the editor's complaints about the system, I surprised them by shifting the conversation to one about streamlining the process of creating new topic pages to quickly respond to current events. Since the request never comes for streamlining processes, the website product manager must be alert to recognizing these patterns in order to shift the discussion to the commonalities.

Streamlining helps for the following reasons:

- It emphasizes outcomes that are good for the business, rather than those that are simply important to the ego of the requester. For example, if creating hot topic pages is important for your business, but that isn't everyone's focus, then by creating a streamlined process you encourage people to create those pages.
- It makes it easier for a wider range of people to undertake the mechanical aspects of achieving the outcome.
- It gives a voice to everyone involved in the activity, so that they can work together to improve the process (rather than creating a one-off that won't get enough attention to improve over time).
- Improvements made to one affect all (even without the active involvement in the previous bullet).
- Decision making is dramatically simplified for everyone (from the requester to the core team that will be implementing the request back to the requester who then will create it in a more streamlined and restricted manner).

There are several ways of streamlining:

- Eliminate steps in a process. For example, if you define minimum standards then you don't have to spend time talking about standards. Rather, you can just check that those standards have been met.
- Reduce the time on steps. For example, if you have defined a form to fill out to request a particular implementation, then there's a lot less time talking about what the requirements are.
- Avoid going through the process at all. Perhaps the best optimization of all is avoiding implementing many requests in the first place, and a clear process can set the standards that mean less (but higher quality) gets implemented.
- Reduce chance of stalling. In a process that is not obvious, it's easy to just stop and forget in the middle. For example, if the content publishing process is not clear and obvious, people may forget where they are, or they may need to wait to follow up with an expert.

New site creation flow

For large web presences, a common problem is the proliferation of sites, often resulting in a large number of sites that are outdated. But having no real strategy means lots of one-offs. If you have a single website, then this section should still be useful in capturing the thought process behind streamlining a common activity. By "site" here we mean either a clearly separate part of the site or a completely different site that is independently managed.

Consider the steps[13] to creating a new website for a large web presence with a suite of sites:

1. **Request.** The process for requesting a subsite
2. **Approve.** The process to approve or reject a site creation
3. **Negotiate.** Negotiating the details, especially the functionality
4. **Train.** Training the team that will be managing the site
5. **Create.** The technical creation of the subsite
6. **Embody.** The site owners adding their content
7. **Review.** Quality review before launch
8. **Launch.** Launching the subsite
9. **Maintain and Innovate.** Ongoing maintenance and innovation across all the subsites (note that continued iteration and improvements happen at this step, over the long term)

When making large changes to a website, for instance in replatforming a big web presence, the time it takes to create sites is essential. See *Website Migration Handbook v2* for more on phasing these sorts of big changes.

On an ongoing basis these steps should be streamlined as well for new sites. The approval step is key, since the best response to a request may be "you could do that with something we already have in place without creating a new site." New sites can quickly create islands of information leading to a disjointed experience for your site visitors, and sometimes sites are requested simply for ego reasons.

Assuming a site has passed the standards required to justify a site creation, there are many ways the process can be streamlined:

- Eliminating steps. Notably, if you have standardized on the requirements for a type of site, then there could be no negotiation.
- Reducing cross-team interactions (for specific requests). If there are

---

13 http://www.realstorygroup.com/Blog/2188-Streamlining-large-multisite-CMS-rollouts

specific minimum standards for a site that are clearly articulated, then the discussion around whether the site should be created could be simplified.

- Reducing the total work for a specific site. For example, a standardized site will take much less time to create than one that is completely one-off.

Types of sites

One of the most important steps in streamlining and rationalizing site creations is considering the different types of site requests you may face, thereby implementing common sites on similar templates. This should be advantageous to everyone since: 1) the site visitor gets more consistency, 2) you're more likely to be able to roll out future features for common sites, and 3) owners of common sites get to work together to make the best possible sites. For a group approach to work, you also need to ensure that you don't let sites get implemented as one-offs that should be part of a natural group.

Some examples of site types (similar to how content can be grouped and templated by content type):

- Specific location (for example a building or campus)
- Country or large geographic area
- Campaign or promotion
- Partnership
- Topic (news topic, research area, disease, etc.)
- Group
- Chapter (of an association for example)
- Organizational unit

I gasped a bit when I wrote that last bullet, since usually organization-based websites are not very effective. But, as with all the types of sites listed above, the point is that you need to think clearly about the different types of sites and how you will handle them.

Should we create this site?

When looking at the request to create a new site, the bar must be very high. Many of the questions to answer will be specific to the type of site (for example, a partnership site will have its own questions), but generically here are some common questions:

- Is this site of a known type? If yes, does it meet type-specific standards (if you don't have such a list defined, then create it)? If no, are you sure?
- Will this site further business goals?
- How will this site be managed over the long haul? Or will it be decommissioned shortly after launch?
- Who will walk through the steps of creating the site?
- Can this be implemented in a way such that all sites of the same type are displayed and maintained in a similar way?
- Is this just a vanity site?

Advanced streamlining

When discussing streamlining, there are two key steps: 1) what is being streamlined, and 2) a specific request of that type. For example, you may be streamlining the creation of new topic pages (#1). Then at some point a specific topic is requested (#2). So for any request for something that comes up frequently, there are these general steps to consider from conception to implementation:

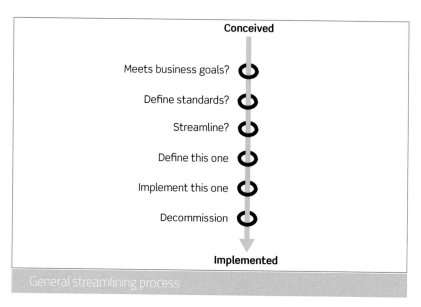

General streamlining process

 Before going any further, of course, just because a specific request is made, and it's easy and streamlined to respond to, doesn't mean that request should be implemented. For instance, some tools make it easy to set up a website, and often the actual implementation of those tools winds up with an explosion of poor websites.

Looking at the steps in more detail:

1. Meets business goals? Does this request even meet basic business objectives?
2. Define standards? Are standards already defined for this sort of request? If yes, have minimum standards already been defined for

this type of request, and does this request meet those standards? If no standards are defined, do we need to define them? After the standards are defined, do you need to implement them in the tool-set so that they are naturally and routinely met?

3. Streamline? Is this a process we should streamline? If it is already streamlined, then use the streamlined process (not treating this request as a one-off).

4. Define this one. When everything is a one-off, then each instance needs to be defined from scratch. But in a streamlined process, in many ways it's just about filling in the blanks of a form.

5. Implement this one. Implement this specific instance.

6. Decommission. Take it offline after it is no longer useful.

In my experience, the common approach is simply, "if it's easy to do, let's do it". For example, if it's easy to create a topic page then simply implement a topic page whenever it is requested (jumping right to numbers 4 and 5 above). But, as discussed in "Small and simple," that sort of explosion of content isn't very helpful.

Sticking with the topic page example, what if you first define minimum standards? For example, let's say that the topic page must have at least 10 content items tagged to that topic and you must always publish on the topic at least every six months (for a richer exploration on topic standards, see "Exploding Topics Pages"[14] on Slideshare). Digging deeper, you may realize there are two types of topics: a) permanent topics that you will always be writing about, and b) news-driven topics that may be very temporary but important for your organization to "cover" in the short term. With that backdrop, you could follow this process:

1. Meets business goals? If it's being considered for a permanent topic, then perhaps you have a deeper review (probably including subject matter expert review) and a higher threshold (for example, a permanent topic may require deeper background information). At any rate, there would be minimum standards as discussed above, and the requester would need to commit to maintaining the minimum standards (both the initial one requiring a certain amount of content, and the ongoing one to publish on the topic at least every six months), and understand the repercussions if not (see the decommission step further on).

14 http://www.slideshare.net/jdavidhobbs/exploding-topics-pages

2. Define standards? In this case, the standards are defined and simply applied.
3. Streamline? This would be a streamlined process.
4. Define this one. Let's assume in this case that there is a form for the requester to fill out, and they do so. Then these parameters are entered into the administrative screens to create the shell of the topic page.
5. Implement. The topic owner would then enter the information needed to meet the minimum standard.
6. Decommission. If any of the minimum standards were not met at some point in the future, then the topic page would be put in an archive state (perhaps not included in the navigation and stamped with a "this topic is no longer actively being covered" warning) automatically.

You just read STREAMLINE COMMON ACTIVITIES.
Now take at least this one action:

What legitimate change should be able to happen much faster (or consistently) than it is now? Take one step toward improving that process.

Summary of Part 3: Ongoing Change

- Some changes should happen quickly, and others should happen slowly. This isn't the same thing as what is easy to implement.
- Streamline routine changes, starting with content publishing. Not only is it important to make common changes easier, it will better standardize the experience for everyone and also free up time for other changes.
- Create space to consider changes that are not routine. This will give you space to carefully consider changes.
- Have a regular and recurring schedule to consider changes, and creatively batch the changes.
- Think beyond "yes" and "no" as responses to requests (in fact, these should be rare responses).

CLOSING
HOW FAR WILL YOU TAKE THIS?

We as an industry are on the cusp of transcending the website as a dumping ground to web presences that must be managed as focused products that serve the business. Product thinking, getting the bones right, and ongoing change are key elements of this. But chances are you aren't prepared to jump into making all the changes needed to do everything in this book. Let's look at how to move forward from wherever you are now as well as some of the skills and activities that should be applied to product management.

> Practice without improvement is meaningless. — Chuck Knox

We covered why focus is important in the introduction, what product management thinking is, and then how to do it (getting the bones right and then doing ongoing changes). Throughout the book, there are "at least do this one thing" suggestions to help push you along for wherever you are now. In closing, let's look some more at how far you will be pushing website product management at your company.

This book describes both how to think of your web presence as a product and techniques for treating it that way. The first step is being aware of the need for focus and thinking long term and broadly. If there is general awareness of these issues, then at least streamline content publishing and have clear rules about one-offs. This will start giving you room to consider bigger improvements. Finally, after you have streamlined content publishing, move into deeper product management. Most notably, have a regular and recurring process to consider and deliver bigger changes.

Here's a scale showing these levels of website product management:

Levels of website product management	
Level	**How you know you're here**
Unaware	<ul><li>Think launching one-offs is a win</li><li>Think your problems are about flexibility</li><li>Not having the discussion about **web-presence-wide** quality</li></ul>
Aware	<ul><li>Generally accepted by the web team(s) that keeping better focus during website change is desirable</li></ul>
Basic product management	<ul><li>Streamlined and standardized common content publishing</li><li>Set rules for consideration of one-offs</li></ul>
Advanced product management	<ul><li>Everyone involved in website management knows that their requests will be evaluated broadly, long term, and against business objectives</li><li>Regular cycle of ongoing improvements</li><li>Other common activities are streamlined</li></ul>
Look at where you are now, and try to improve from there.	

Where are you on this scale now? When deciding whether your organization is aware of the need for website product management, note that this awareness needs to be generally accepted, and that there at least needs to be a discussion about quality across your entire web presence (not just your particular silo or slice of the web). Obviously I recommend that you pass this book around your organization to raise awareness, but if you are attempting to raise awareness then I recommend taking two steps:

1. Streamline and standardize common content publishing. This will not only have an impact on the organization, but also show that you are serious about making improvements.
2. Set rules to consider one-offs. Even if, for whatever reason, you can't stop the locomotive coming at you (perhaps from the top of the organization) for a one-off, clearly documenting the disadvantages (or perhaps advantages) will at least ensure that people briefly pause to consider the advantages. This approach could be extended to any change of questionable value. This noting of issues will both establish that you are thinking about these broader issues, and also help to start the discussion.

If nothing else, ask more product questions.

If you do nothing else, ask more product questions (about the business need and long-term / broad impacts).

Product management skills

The blend of skills for product management is unique, and some of the most important skills are:

- Business and technology smarts
- Ability to think broadly and deeply
- Thick skin and able to make decisions
- Creativity, and the ability to transcend the specific request
- Positivity and the ability to articulate a compelling vision

Business and technology smarts

As mentioned elsewhere, I'm not necessarily advocating for everyone to start aspiring to call themselves a website product manager, but there is value in someone having all these skills. In particular, there is extremely high value in having someone who both:

107

- Understands the business
- Understands the technology

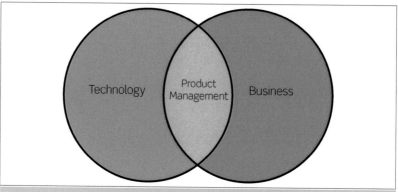

Product management focuses where technology and business meet.

I remember a colleague of mine when I was a product manager at the World Bank. I was going to a meeting with a variety of testy clients. During the meeting, we discussed various options of dealing with some of their concerns, and I assured them that for one issue we could implement things the way we had discussed in the meeting. My colleague was upset with me as we left the meeting, saying, "Why didn't you tell me before the meeting we were planning on implementing that?" To which I replied: "There was no plan to implement that before we walked into that meeting, but during the meeting we discussed a way that I'm sure will be trivial for the technical team to implement". Fundamentally, I knew enough of the business and the technology to, on the spot, steer toward reasonable requirements. No need for several meetings, bringing in a variety of technical team members, and generally disrupting everyone's schedule.

As should be clear at this point in the handbook, your job isn't to do exactly what the client asks. In fact, if you do everything that everyone asks, something is almost certainly wrong (for instance, you'll end up with an inconsistent system that is difficult to maintain). You should know the system as well as any user, and also know the other requests that users have made. With that background, you can quickly respond intelligently and creatively to issues that clients raise in meetings or even hallways (rather than having to go back to the technical team all the time). You'll be able to suggest alternate approaches that satisfy more users, are more stable, or help the person more constructively.

Skills or talents?

One of the goals of this book is to encourage everyone involved in running a website to step up and treat their web presence as a product that needs to be maintained for high quality over time. For a variety of roles many authors have argued that innate talents are more important than learned skills, and in particular Roger Cauvin has written in his blog post "Talents of Great Product Managers" that generic talents are more important than skills for product managers. As the above World Bank example illustrates, sometimes having technology, business, and domain experience coupled with relevant talents is particularly powerful. In general, although the list here encompasses skills (implying that they can be learned), you will be most effective if each is grounded in an underlying predisposition or skill.

Ability to think broadly and deeply

Someone could have business and technology smarts but still think in a silo. In fact, this way of thinking is fairly common, and actually encouraged by various disciplines and organizations. But remember that a key element of product management is to look broadly at the success of your web presence. However, it isn't enough to just look broadly. The details are where quality emerges on the site. Of course, when managing the website as a product we rely on other players in the organization to actually execute, and even to define many of the details. But we cannot just let the details happen. We must constantly be alert and dive into the mind-numbing details where necessary to deliver a high-quality product.

Thick skin and able to make decisions

Much of product management is making decisions, and, as stated above, frequently you are not implementing literally what people request. Hopefully the additional thinking and perspective that product management brings will usually mean requesters are even more pleased with the results, but obviously many people will be disappointed. Someone who wants to quickly say "yes" to all changes will probably create a situation where nothing can get done (and the site becomes unfocused). So in the end a thick skin is an absolute requirement.

Creativity, and the ability to transcend the specific request

As should be obvious in all the examples in this book, product management must shift the conversation, creatively interpreting requests for their underlying need to define solutions that are not obvious (until they are proposed, at which point they may seem that way). Product management cannot be literal in taking requests, and must quickly think of different ways of approaching problems.

Positivity and the ability to articulate a compelling vision

Although a thick skin is required, at the root the website product management must be positive and able to articulate a compelling vision. In many ways, this is what the website needs to be "sold." In particular, nothing will ever be perfect, and people will constantly be pointing out those imperfect elements to you. So product management needs to retain a positive attitude to encourage people to continue working on the website.

Product management activities

There are three primary product management activities:

- Defining and pushing through the work program (throughout the lifecycle)
- Streamlining common activities
- Pushing through requirements to get the maximum business value out of the site

Yes, those are also the last three chapters of this handbook, so here we will break them down together in more of a month-by-month outline. But first, all of the above activities boil down to a combination of 1) definition and 2) discussion. When product managing the web presence, you must be ready and able to synthesize everything heard in order to take the stand (and hits). Furthermore, product management is going to be talking with a lot of people (but not in endless discussions, as noted above). If you have a recurring three-month work program, then the month-by-month activities may be:

Example: product management activities by month	
Month One: Implementation	■ Refining requirements as needed ■ Background discussions on longer-range issues or those that couldn't be put in the current plan
Month Two: Clarifying requests	■ Diving into requests with the requesters to better understand the requests ■ Meeting with relevant stakeholders (other than requesters) to further explore requirements ■ Working with technical team to develop rough cut effort estimates ■ Working with technical team to discuss background technical, maintenance, and security issues that may need to be in the work program ■ Working with other delivery groups (especially training and helpdesk) to understand issues that are arising
Month Three: Defining the work program	■ Define work program, especially by working with all the delivery teams to ensure it can be implemented. ■ Communicate work program
The exact sequence will depend on your process, but this example represents the types of product management activities on an ongoing basis.	

Also, throughout the process, when taking a product view, we need to shepard through implementation of the work program that has already been communicated and committed.

> **You just read HOW FAR WILL YOU TAKE THIS?**
> **Now take at least this one action:**
>
> Attempt to deepen how you approach website product management at your organization, in particular by figuring out where you are in the table listing levels of product management and take steps toward the next level.

Book summary

- Focus is important, and you can help to focus your web presence.
- Think of your web presence as a product, and in particular think long term and broadly.
- Instead of thinking about launches, concentrate on getting the bones right. In particular, work to maximize impact and collaborate for better requirements.
- Be prepared for ongoing change, including regularly phasing in changes and streamlining common activities.
- Wherever you are now, you can do more to treat your web presence as a product.

Reading List

Many of these resources are specifically referenced in the text, but all are useful in thinking of your web presence as a product. This list is very interdisciplinary, which is part of the point of product management.

- Cauvin (blog), Roger Cauvin
- Content Here (blog), Seth Gottleib
- CMS Myth (blog), Jeff Cram and others
- *Content Strategy for the Web (2nd Edition)*, Kristina Halvorson and Melissa Rach, 2012.
- *Design in Nature: How the Constructal Law Governs Evolution in Biology, Physics, Technology, and Social Organization*, Adrian Bejan, 2013.
- *Focus: The Future of Your Company Depends On It*, Al Ries, 2005.
- Gadgetopia (blog), Deane Barker.
- *Living with Complexity*, Donald A. Norman, 2010.
- *Mastering the Requirements Process: Getting Requirements Right (3rd Edition)*, Suzanne Robertson and James Robertson, 2012.
- *Maximum Engagement*, David Gammel, 2011.
- *The Mythical Man-Month (2nd Edition)*, Frederick P. Brooks, Jr., 1995.
- *The Product Manager's Desk Reference*, Steven Haines, 2008.
- *The Product Manager's Handbook Fourth Edition*, Linda Gorcheis, 2011.
- Real Story Group blog, Real Story Group.
- *Simple and Usable Web, Mobile, and Interaction Design*, Giles Colborne, 2010.
- *Simple: Conquering the Crisis of Complexity*, Alan Siegel and Irene Etzkorn, 2013.
- *Software Requirements 3*, Karl E Wiegers and Joy Beatty, 2013.
- *The Stranger's Long Neck*, Gerry McGovern (also subscribe to his weekly newsletter). 2010.
- Tyner Blain (blog), Scott Sehlhorst
- *Website Migration Handbook v2*, David Hobbs, 2011.
- WelchmanPierpoint blog, WelchmanPierpoint.

Made in the USA
San Bernardino, CA
25 November 2014